Object-Oriented Design

Object-Oriented Design

Peter Coad and Edward Yourdon

YOURDON Press
Prentice Hall Building
Englewood Cliffs, New Jersey 07632

Library of Congress Cataloging-in-Publication Data

Coad, Peter.
    Object-oriented design / Peter Coad and Edward Yourdon.
        p.   cm. -- (Yourdon Press computing series)
    Includes bibliographical references and index.
    ISBN 0-13-630070-7
    1. System analysis. 2. Software engineering.   I. Yourdon,
Edward. II. Title. III. Series.
T57.6.C62 1991
005.1--dc20   91-9376
                                                                  CIP

Editorial/production supervision: MARY P. ROTTINO
Manufacturing buyer: KELLY BEHR/SUSAN BRUNKE
Photos by: DON ROGERS PHOTOGRAPHY—Austin, Texas USA
All OOD drawings in this text were developed using Object International's OODTool™.

Published by Prentice-Hall, Inc.
A Simon & Schuster Company
Englewood Cliffs, New Jersey 07632

The publisher offers discounts on this book when ordered
in bulk quantities. For more information, write:
        Special Sales/College Marketing
        College Technical and Reference Division
        Prentice Hall
        Englewood Cliffs, New Jersey 07632

OOWorkbench™, OOATool™, OODTool™, OOCodeGen™ and The Coad Letter™ are
trademarks of Object International, Inc.
OOAdvisor® is a registered trademark of Object International, Inc.
Smalltalk/V® is a registered trademark of Digitalk, Inc.
ObjectPlus™ is a trademark of Easyspec, Inc.
Prograph™ is a trademark of TGS Systems, Inc.
Adagen™ is a trademark of Mark V Systems, Ltd.
Apple®, Macintosh®, and MacApp® are registered trademarks of Apple Computer, Inc.
IBM® is a registered trademark of International Business Machines.

Printed in the United States of America

10 9 8 7 6 5 4 3 2 1

ISBN 0-13-630070-7

Prentice-Hall International (UK) Limited, *London*
Prentice-Hall of Australia Pty. Limited, *Sydney*
Prentice-Hall Canada Inc., *Toronto*
Prentice-Hall Hispanoamericana, S.A., *Mexico*
Prentice-Hall of India Private Limited, *New Delhi*
Prentice-Hall of Japan, Inc., *Tokyo*
Simon & Schuster Asia Pte. Ltd., *Singapore*
Editora Prentice-Hall do Brasil, Ltda., *Rio de Janeiro*

Dedication

To Mom and Dad.
With love,
PC

To Toni, Jenny, Jamie, and David.
Thanks for putting up with yet another book project.

EY

Contents

Preface

OOD—object-oriented design—is a relatively young method. We are committed to the continued development of OOD—in practice and in writing.

This second volume in a series of guides to object-oriented development focuses on these critical topics:

Improving Design. Chapter 1 presents principles for managing complexity, the role of prototyping, and the objectives, motivations, and benefits of OOD.

Developing the Multilayer, Multicomponent Model. Chapter 2 investigates discovery of a model, a continuum of representation, five layers (and five activities), four components (and four additional activities), and notations.

Designing the Problem Domain Component. Chapter 3 presents strategies for improving OOA results and applying specific criteria for adding to OOA results during OOD.

Designing the Human Interaction Component. Chapter 4 adds to the design strategy with: classifying the humans, describing the humans and their task scenarios, designing the command hierarchy, designing the detailed interaction, continuing to prototype, designing the needed classes, and accounting for graphical user interfaces.

Designing the Task Management Component. Chapter 5 adds strategies to support real-time tasking, including: identifying event-driven tasks, clock-driven tasks, priority tasks, and critical tasks; identifying a coordinator; challenging each task; and defining each task.

Designing the Data Management Component. Chapter 6 brings in strategies for assessing data management approaches and tools, designing the data layout, and designing the corresponding Services.

Applying OOD with OOPLs (or Less than an OOPL). Chapter 7 takes a pragmatic look at programming languages. The chapter features detailed examples for selected OOPLs (C++, Object Pascal, Smalltalk, Objective-C, Eiffel) plus "less than OOPLs" (Ada and C). The chapter concludes with a section on selecting OOPLs.

Applying OOD Criteria. Chapter 8 presents a wide variety of design trade-off and evaluation criteria, including: interaction coupling, inheritance coupling, Service cohesion, Class cohesion, generalization-specialization cohesion, reuse, and others.

Selecting CASE for OOD. Chapter 9 investigates CASE: what is needed and what is available. We used a CASE tool for the examples in this book. The book includes a business reply card, offering a small project version of OOD*Tool*™, available at nominal cost. With this, we continue to establish a trend for other authors to follow: here's a method *and* an inexpensive tool—to accelerate the method into practice.

Getting Started with OOD. Chapter 10 addresses key issues related to introducing OOD into an organization.

We enthusiastically thank Prentice Hall and its staff for the opportunity to produce this book.

Peter Coad
Object International, Inc.
Austin, Texas
USA

Edward Yourdon
New York City, New York
USA

Acknowledgments

This book would not exist if it were not for the kind help of many people, including those specifically acknowledged here.

First, we thank our clients, who have extended to us both challenges and kindness. We remain most grateful.

From Peter: Special thanks to Don Callahan (Bell Labs), Charles Pitcher and Al Woolfrey (Canadian Imperial Bank of Commerce), Chris Doylend and Shane Warnez (Mitel Corporation), Christer Hoberg and Mats Weidmar (Enea Data, Sweden), and Mark Mitchell and Tom Huchel (Technology Training Corp.).

Between the two of us, we speak in about two dozen countries per year. We thank and acknowledge those persistent seminar delegates who have helped us to refine and clarify our work.

We thank and acknowledge how much we learned and benefited from the designers we studied, especially those who allowed us very close scrutiny of themselves, their designs, and their programming, including:

Reed Phillips and selected team members—Sam Adams, Ken Auer, Steve Burbeck, S. Sridahr (Knowledge Systems, Inc.);

Jeff McKenna (McKenna Consulting Group); and

Hermann Schindler (Advance Micro Devices) and Larry Marran (Hewlett-Packard).

We also thank Object International, Inc., for allowing us to use one of their commercial software products, OOA*Tool*™, as a case study in this book.

We're grateful to Ragan Wilkinson for assisting in developing the programming language examples.

And we remain very thankful to our reviewers, each helping to make this book a much better result:

Sam Adams (Knowledge Systems Corporation)
John Henson (Ralph Kirkley Associates)
Tom Jenson (Hughes Aircraft Company)
Jeff McKenna (McKenna Consulting Group)
Ron Norman (San Diego State University)
Mats Weidmar (Enea Data, Sweden)
Bill Wiley (Taylor University)

And special thanks to the production team—the often unsung heros of producing a readable book. Thanks to Paul Becker, Mary Rottino, and Noreen Regina (Prentice Hall) and Francis Morgan and the staff at Morgan-Cain & Associates (Tucson, Arizona USA).

0

Introduction

This book is a companion to our book on *Object-Oriented Analysis*. The material in both books is based upon the concepts of objects and attributes, wholes and parts, and classes and members.

As the *Encyclopaedia Britannica* points out:

> In apprehending the real world, men [people] constantly employ three methods of organization, which pervade all of their thinking:
>
> (1) the differentiation of experience into particular objects and their attributes—e.g., when they distinguish between a tree and its size or spatial relations to other objects,
>
> (2) the distinction between whole objects and their component parts—e.g., when they contrast a tree with its component branches, and
>
> (3) the formation of and the distinction between different classes of objects—e.g., when they form the class of all trees and the class of all stones and distinguish between them.
>
> [*Encyclopaedia Britannica*, "Classification Theory," 1986]

The notation and approach of OOD builds upon these three constantly employed methods of organization.

This book is aimed at the practicing software engineer, the person who has to tackle real-world systems development projects every day. We assume that readers are concerned with the "middle" part of the development cycle: the activity of *design*. A designer may also be involved in the front-end activities of interviewing users to determine system requirements, as well as being involved in the back-end issues of coding and system testing. But in this book, we are speaking primarily to the person responsible for developing the overall software architecture for a system.

Managers, testers, standard-bearers, and programmers can also read this book and expect to profit from the overall approach to improving systems design. However, the book is *not* intended to be read by end-users; this group would profit instead by reading our companion book, *Object-Oriented Analysis*.

0.1 HISTORY

Why has the "object paradigm" finally come of age? Why now?

Object-oriented *programming* was first discussed in the late 1960s by the SIMULA community. By the early 1970s, it was an important part of the Smalltalk language developed at Xerox PARC. Meanwhile, the rest of the world bumbled along with languages like COBOL and FORTRAN and used functional decomposition methods to address problems of design and implementation. Little, if any, discussion focused on object-oriented *design*, and virtually none on object-oriented *analysis*.

Four changes have occurred over the past decade and are now key factors as we continue in the 1990s:

- The underlying concepts of an object-oriented approach in the software field have had over two decades to mature, and attention has gradually shifted from issues of coding to issues of design and analysis.
- The underlying technology for building systems has become much more powerful. Ideas about design are influenced by preconceived ideas about how one would write code; and ideas about coding are strongly influenced by the programming language one has available. It was difficult to think about structured programming when the languages of choice were assembler and FORTRAN; things became easier with Pascal, PL/1, and ALGOL. Similarly, it was difficult to think about coding in an object-oriented fashion when the language of choice was COBOL or plain-vanilla C; it has become easier with C++ and Smalltalk.
- The systems built today are different from what they were ten or twenty years ago: they are larger, more complex, and more volatile. An object-oriented approach to analysis and design is likely to lead to a more stable system. Also, today's on-line, interactive systems devote much more attention to the *user interface* than the text-oriented batch processing systems of the 1970s. An object-oriented approach to such systems—from analysis through design and into coding—is a more natural way of dealing with such user-oriented systems.
- The systems built today are more "domain-oriented" than the systems built in the 1970s and 1980s. Functional complexity is less

of a concern than it was before; modeling the data has become a moderate priority; modeling problem domain understanding and system responsibilities take higher priority.

0.2 METHOD AND TOOL

With this book, we'd like to continue a trend set in the OOA book: present a method *and* a low-cost drawing-and-checking tool to try it out. The tool presented in this book is OOD*Tool*™. [1]

To provide you with a *small project version* of OOD*Tool*™ at nominal cost, Peter has included a business reply card in this book (if the card is gone, please write for details). Send the card to Peter Coad at Object International, Inc., 3202 W. Anderson Lane, Suite 208-724, Austin, Texas 78757-1022, USA.

All examples in this book were developed using OOA*Tool*™ and an early version of OOD*Tool*™.

0.3 FUTURE ADVANCES

OOD and its companion, OOA, are relatively young methods; they will continue to evolve in practice. So we suggest that you use this book as a starting point for applying OOD—tailoring and expanding the method to suit your specific organization or project needs.

To provide you with periodic updates on OOA and OOD, Peter includes with this book a business reply card offering free special reports called *The Coad Letter*™: *New Advances in Object-Oriented Analysis and Design* (if the card is gone, please write for details). Send the card to Peter Coad at Object International, Inc., 3202 W. Anderson Lane, Suite 208-724, Austin, Texas 78757-1022, USA.

In addition, ongoing developments in OOA and OOD are discussed in Ed Yourdon's monthly software journal, *American Programmer*. For a complimentary sample issue, contact Ed Yourdon at American Programmer, Inc., Dept. 13, 161 West 86th Street, New York, NY 10024-3411.

1

Improving Design

This chapter presents basic terminology, principles for managing complexity, the impact of prototyping, objectives, and motivations and benefits of object-oriented design (OOD).

1.1 BASIC TERMINOLOGY

The title *Object-Oriented Design* indicates that this book has something to do with *objects* and with *design*.

Let's start with basic terminology. First, the ubiquitous terms *object* and *class*:

From the dictionary:

Object. [something thrown in the way (Medieval Latin), a casting before (Latin)] A person or thing to which action, thought, or feeling is directed. Anything visible or tangible; a material product or substance.

Class. [a division of the Roman people (Latin); a calling, summons (Greek)] A number of people or things grouped together because of certain likenesses or common traits.

[*Webster's*, 1977]

And more specifically, for OOD:

Object. An *abstraction* of something in the domain of a problem or its implementation, reflecting the capabilities of a system to keep information about it, interact with it, or both; an *encapsulation* of Attribute values and their exclusive Services. (Synonym: an Instance.)

Class. A description of one or more Objects, describable with a uniform set of Attributes and Services; in addition, it may describe how to create new Objects in the Class.

Class-&-Object. A term meaning "a Class and the Objects in that Class."

In OOD, the primary motivation for identifying Class-&-Objects is to match the technical representation of a system more closely to a conceptual view of a problem domain and its implementation domain.

Next, the terms *analysis* and *design*:
From the dictionary:

Analysis. [dissolving, a resolution of a whole into parts (Greek)] A separating or breaking up of any whole into its parts so as to find out their nature, proportion, function, relationship, etc.

Design. [a marking out (Latin)] The making of original plans, sketches, patterns, etc.

[derived from *Webster's*, 1977]

And more specifically:

Analysis. The practice of studying a problem domain, leading to a specification of externally observable behavior; a complete, consistent, and feasible statement of what is needed; a coverage of both functional and quantified operational characteristics (e.g., reliability, availability, performance).

Design. The practice of taking a specification of externally observable behavior and adding details needed for actual computer system implementation, including human interaction, task management, and data management details.

This book is about *design*, not *analysis*. While the systems analyst is concerned explicitly with the user's world, with the problem/application domain, and the system's "essential" responsibilities, the designer is concerned with the job of moving analysis results (e.g., a specification) into a particular hardware/software implementation.

Subsequent chapters demonstrate a graphical notation for OOD; they also show how such a design can be organized into four major components: a Problem Domain Component, a Human Interaction Component, a Task Management Component, and a Data Management Component. But before delving into those details, this initial chapter summarizes some of the fundamental principles, the impact of prototyping, key objectives, and the motivations and benefits of OOD.

1.2 PRINCIPLES FOR MANAGING COMPLEXITY

Principles for managing complexity—pertinent to object-oriented analysis (OOA) and OOD—include the following:

- Abstraction
    Procedural
    Data
- Encapsulation
- Inheritance (portraying Generalization-Specialization)
- Association
- Communication with messages
- Pervading methods of organization
    Objects and attributes
    Whole and parts
    Classes and members, and distinguishing between them
- Scale
- Behavior classification
    Immediate causation
    Change over time
    Similarity of functions

1.2.1 Abstraction

One principle is abstraction:

Abstraction. The principle of ignoring those aspects of a subject that are not relevant to the current purpose in order to concentrate more fully on those that are. [*Oxford*, 1986]

When one uses abstraction, one admits that a real-world artifact is complex; rather than try to comprehend the entire thing, one selects only part of it.

Procedural abstraction is often characterized as "function/subfunction" abstraction. Breaking processing down into substeps is one basic method of handling complexity. But using such a breakdown for organizing a design is somewhat arbitrary and highly volatile. (Procedural abstraction is not the primary form of abstraction for OOD; however, it does come into play within the limited context of specifying and describing Services.)

Another, more powerful abstraction mechanism is data abstraction. This principle can be a basis for organization of thinking and of specification of a system's responsibilities.

Data Abstraction. The principle of defining a data type in terms of the operations that apply to objects of the type, with the constraint that the values of such objects can be modified and observed only by the use of the operations. [*Oxford*, 1986]

In applying data abstraction, a designer can define Attributes and Services that exclusively manipulate those Attributes. The only way to get to the Attributes is via a Service. Attributes and their Services may be treated as an intrinsic whole.

1.2.2 Encapsulation

Another principle is encapsulation:

Encapsulation (Information Hiding). A principle, used when developing an overall program structure, that each component of a program should encapsulate or hide a single design decision... The interface to each module is defined in such a way as to reveal as little as possible about its inner workings. [*Oxford*, 1986]

Encapsulation helps minimize rework when developing a new system. If a designer encapsulates the parts of the analysis effort that are most volatile, then the (inevitably) changing requirements become less of a threat. Encapsulation keeps related content together; it minimizes traffic between different parts of the work; and it separates certain specified requirements from other parts of the specification that may use those requirements.

Note that data abstraction is one form of the "keep related things together" aspect of encapsulation. Also note that communication with messages (described later in this chapter) is one form of the "narrow interface" aspect of encapsulation.

1.2.3 Inheritance (Portraying Generalization-Specialization)

Inheritance is another underlying principle:

Inheritance. A mechanism for expressing similarity among Classes, simplifying definition of Classes similar to one(s) previously defined. It portrays generalization and specialization, making common Attributes and Services explicit within a Class hierarchy or lattice.

This principle forms the basis for a significant technique of explicit expression of commonality. Inheritance allows a designer to specify common Attributes and Services once, as well as to specialize and extend those Attributes and Services into specific cases. Inheritance may be applied to explicitly express commonality, beginning with the early activities of analysis, and continuing in design.

1.2.4 Association

Another principle is association.

Association. The union or connection of ideas.
[*Webster's*, 1977]

People use association to tie together certain things that happen at a particular time or under similar circumstances; e.g., tying together a vehicle and an owner, a clerk and a legal event.

1.2.5 Communication with Messages

Webster's defines a message as follows:

Message. Any communication, written or oral, sent between persons.
[*Webster's*, 1977]

A principle—notably for interfaces—is communication with messages. It's related to encapsulation, in that the details of the action to be performed are encapsulated within the receiver of a message.

1.2.6 Pervading Methods of Organization

Encyclopaedia Britannica says the following about how people organize their thinking:

In apprehending the real world, men [people] constantly employ three methods of organization, which pervade all of their thinking:

(1) the differentiation of experience into particular objects and their attributes—e.g., when they distinguish between a tree and its size or spatial relations to other objects,

(2) the distinction between whole objects and their component parts—e.g., when they contrast a tree with its component branches,

(3) the formation of and the distinction between different classes of objects—e.g., when they form the class of all trees and the class of all stones and distinguish between them.

[*Encyclopaedia Britannica*, "Classification Theory," 1986]

It is worth noting that there are indeed *three* pervading methods of organization—not just one. In practice, applying "objects and attributes," "whole and parts," *and* "classes, members, and distinguishing between them" provides significantly greater insights into a problem domain and a system's responsibilities than applying only "objects and attributes."

1.2.7 Scale

A principle that applies the whole-part principle to help an observer relate to something very large—without being overwhelmed—is called "scale":

When the proportions of architectural composition are applied to a particular building, the two-termed relationship of the parts to the whole must be harmonized with a third term—the observer. This three-termed relationship is called scale.

[*Encyclopaedia Britannica*, "Architecture, The Art of," 1986]

With scale, notation and strategy can include ways to guide a reader through a larger OOD model.

1.2.8 Behavior Classification

Shortly after finding the "pervading methods of organization" statement, someone asked, "Yes, but what about the active side of objects—what of their behavior?" Having benefited from *Encyclopaedia Britannica* before, we turned to it once again:

Three types of behavior classification are used most commonly:

(1) on the basis of immediate causation,

(2) on similarity of evolutionary history [change over time], and

(3) on the similarity of function.

[*Encyclopaedia Britannica*, "Animal Behaviour," 1986]

A major advance in the 1980s was the addition of an event-response strategy to structured analysis; this was an application of the first of these three categories of behavior.

1.3 OOD AND THE IMPACT OF PROTOTYPING

Why prototype?

> To build a working demonstration for feedback from the users
>
> To have something to play with, something more tangible than drawings of boxes on a piece of paper
>
> To discover early where the hard parts of the system will be

As Jeff McKenna observes, "I try to find out what I don't know, because I know that I can design and program what I do know." Some additional reasons are described below.

1.3.1 Reasons for Prototyping

There are five important reasons for prototyping:

> Because it is dynamic
>
> To experiment with the human interaction component of the design
>
> To discover missing requirements
>
> To test the design
>
> To deliver functionality as early as possible

Prototyping is dynamic. Most object-oriented prototyping tools are relatively new—and come equipped with prototyping capabilities more powerful than the prototyping tools available in the 1970s. OOD prototyping tools may be at odds with your organization's "systems development cycle," in which case the best you can do is use the prototyping tools to carry out the antiquated development cycle activities a little bit faster and more easily.

But gradually prototyping tools are changing the way people build systems. For many, prototyping is the natural way to work. Nobody today would suggest that programs should be developed by keypunching cards and overnight batch compilation; interactive source program development—whether from a dumb terminal or a smart workstation—is now the norm, the dynamic way to compose programs. Prototyping tools simply takes this concept a step further.

Prototyping helps experiment with the human interface. Bill Curtis argues that the 1990s will be the "decade of the human interface." User-friendly interfaces are a key to the acceptability of a new system. In the 1980s, this simply meant designing on-line screens with proper attention to color, underlining, reverse video, blinking fields, etc. Today, it means pull-down menus, pop-up windows, mouse input, icons, and all the other components of a graphical user interface.

However, the current generation of more than three million software developers around the world is relatively inexperienced with GUI environments; and the vast army of end-users is even less experienced. Users have a difficult time describing the human interface they want—except, perhaps, to say, "Make it like a Macintosh!" And system developers have a hard time explaining, with words or diagrams, the "look and feel" of the human interface.

In the 1980s, developers could provide a static simulation of the user interface using screen painters; they were hardly more sophisticated than the screen layouts people laboriously drew by hand in the 1970s, but at least they showed where to expect the color and the blinking cursor.

But today's GUI environment cannot be realistically modeled in a static fashion. The user has to see the interface *in motion*. You might buy a bicycle by looking at a picture, but you wouldn't buy a car without a test drive; for today's computer users, the equivalent of a test drive is prototyping.

Prototyping helps discover missing requirements. If the problem domain is well understood, and *if* the requirements analysis method is an effective one, and *if* the users and analysts communicate effectively, a requirements model may be accurate, ready for submission to the designers and programmers. Unfortunately, these three "ifs" are problematical: the problem domain may be poorly understood; the requirements analysis method may not be the best; and the users and analysts may be unable to communicate.

The traditional answer to this problem, as suggested in Fred Brooks's *The Mythical Man-Month*, was "build one to throw away." But that option is rarely acceptable today. There are only two choices: omniscience (build a complete system from a formal, abstract model—and hope it works) or continual prototyping throughout analysis and design.

Prototyping helps test candidate designs. With ever more powerful hardware, some developers have the luxury of ignoring hardware performance issues—especially for single-user applications that run on a dedicated workstation.

However, performance concerns will never disappear altogether. Even on a dedicated workstation serving a single user, some design approaches may prove to be grossly inadequate. An architecture that looks elegant may suddenly mushroom into a 128-megabyte RAM requirement; a search algorithm that looks particularly clever on paper may suddenly lead to an on-line response time of 15 minutes.

If there are any concerns about hardware performance, prototyping is a good way of getting early warning signals.

Prototyping helps deliver working pieces earlier. The system developer sometimes is under intense pressure to deliver some, if not all, of the functionality of a system at an early date. A conservative development life cycle is at odds with this political situation: by the time the project team has finished its formal analysis and design activities, a frustrated end-user may have canceled the project.

A prototyping approach may deliver some useful functionality that the end-user can put into production. This option must be exercised with caution, though, because early prototypes are almost always devoid of backup and recovery facilities, audit trails, security mechanisms, and other "boring" operational capabilities.

Prototyping can provide political credibility, ranging from a "proof of concept" that the systems design actually works, to a "proof of competency" that the project team is actually capable of getting something accomplished. Even if the full-scale system is not delivered any sooner, the political benefit can be invaluable.

1.3.2 Advice for OOD Prototyping

Keep these points in mind:

Do formal OOA.

And prototype all along the way.

Continue with formal OOD.

And prototype all along the way.

Prototype design components during OOD.

Do formal OOA. Do not abandon altogether the effort to develop a formal model of end-user requirements. As your projects grow ever larger, there will be more of a need to develop an overall *framework* within which to build your prototype. Perhaps you could begin prototyping a simple order-entry system on the first day of the project, but you would not start prototyping a large, complex airline reservation system on the first day.

The amount of time and the level of detail to give to the OOA model will depend, of course, on the factors discussed above. But don't think that your organization's acceptance of prototyping gives you an excuse for avoiding effective and much-needed OOA work.

Continue with formal OOD. Prototyping should not be an excuse for avoiding a formal design effort. A prototype provides a dynamic simulation of a system, which has a number of benefits. But the external appearance of the system—that is, the human interface—provides little information about the internal architecture. And the implementation of the prototype does not provide a perspective on the software architectural details (e.g., "How are the components interconnected, and what happens if I make a change?") that the designer is so interested in.

Thus, we strongly recommend that the designer take the OOA specifications and prototypes and continue them within OOD.

CASE tool support helps greatly in this effort, from OOA to OOD to object-oriented programming (OOP).

Prototype design components. A prototype can provide functionality in one or more of the design components that are discussed in subsequent chapters. Consider prototyping in the following order:

Prototype the Problem Domain Component. As you learn more about the problem domain and the system's responsibilities, this will help you to continue to improve this component.

Prototype the Human Interaction Component. There's no point prototyping windows and pop-up menus until you know what the essential objects and interactions are.

Prototype the Data Management Component. In the early prototypes, you will be dealing with small amounts of data that can be kept in tables or in RAM memory. With the two preceding "foundation" components working well, you should start prototyping with larger amounts of data; this will necessitate a prototype of the data management portion of your system.

Prototype the Task Management Component. Even if the eventual system requires multitasking or some form of real-time behavior, it's important to get the key non-real-time, single-task portions operating first.

There may be variations on this strategy, depending on the kind of system you are building. There is nothing wrong with modifying this strategy, as long as you have a strategy and know which component you are prototyping at any given moment.

1.4 THE KEY OBJECTIVES OF OOD

The key objectives of OOD are to improve productivity, to increase quality, and to elevate maintainability.

1.4.1 Improve Productivity

OOD focuses effort on the up-front activity of software design. In return for this investment, less time is required for testing and defect removal. But the overall productivity improvement during the development of a system may be a modest 20 percent, or even less if the project team is relatively unfamiliar with OOD.

But there is another perspective: instead of improving just the productivity of development, how about improving productivity across the entire life cycle! Most organizations recognize that 75 to 80 percent of a system's cost occurs *after* it has been deployed; this also means that many of the defects are discovered after deployment, and, even more important, *much of the functionality of the system is added after initial deployment*. Thus, a method that emphasizes maintenance improves enterprise productivity by enabling maintenance programmers to make modifications more quickly. This may not impress the end-user who wants a new system developed quickly, but the organization may be able to reduce the number of people assigned to pure maintenance work and free up some for new development work.

OOD can also improve productivity by providing a practical mechanism to *reuse* Classes from one project to another. This is usually implemented with a "Class library" that contains hierarchies of classes and subclasses. The Class library thus becomes a capital investment for the organization. For the first OOD project—where such a Class library may not exist—there is little opportunity for reuse. But after a few years of building and refining a Class library, as a result of dozens of projects, the Class library can provide startling improvements in productivity. New systems are seen increasingly as extension or refinement of Classes already in the library.

1.4.2 Increase Quality

The enormous emphasis on productivity has obscured the need for improvements in software *quality*. The pervasive lack of warranties for PC-based software is an example of the profession's inability to produce products with a known level of quality. But we ignore quality at our peril as systems grow more complex, and as the consequences of software failures grow more serious.

There are many tools, techniques, and methods for improving software quality. However, many organizations rely on slogans or meticulous testing of the *product* (the software itself) at the end of the development process, rather than focusing attention on the *process*. Processes that produce high-quality products early in development—especially analysis and design—can greatly reduce errors discovered later in development and can dramatically improve system quality.

Software quality will take on a new meaning in the 1990s, especially as the worldwide software industry becomes more competitive. As "hard" defects in a software system fall below some threshold, end-users equate "quality" with more than just the absence of defects. Software quality—fitness for use—begins to include ease of use, portability, and ease of modification. Thus, maintainability and the ability of a system to deal with continual change, will become more important aspects of software quality in the future.

1.4.3 Elevate Maintainability

The requirements for a system will always be in a state of flux. Management may impose an artificial freezing of requirements at a particular point in time. But the true requirements, the needed system, will continue to evolve. Many forces affect this ever-changing requirements set: clients, competition, regulators, approvers, and technologists.

A designer endeavors to organize a design so that it is resilient to change; a packaging that will remain stable over time is sought. But *how* can the designer organize a design to accommodate changes that cannot even be anticipated over a period of years or decades? The answer is to separate those parts of the system that are intrinsically volatile from those parts that are likely to be stable.

What is the impact of additions, extensions, changes, and deletions of features in a system design? This is especially important when considering "families" of systems—that is, situations where a variety of implementations may be needed. Stability is also important throughout the development of a system, when over-optimistic goals need to be toned down from a full implementation to a lesser system.

Regardless of the method, a software design must eventually address processing. In an object-oriented development approach, Services will be needed to create an Object, connect an Object to other Objects, calculate a result, and provide ongoing monitoring. The degree of Service sophistication is quite volatile; such sophistication is continually subject to the quadruple constraint—capability, schedule, budget, and people.

The designer does not avoid specifying Services; nor can designing a required Service be avoided. This work must always be done. The important consideration is: What comes first? What predominates? What is most stable over time?

External interfaces are the next most likely components to change. How smart or dumb are the devices? What do other systems need from the system under consideration? What does this system need from others? What requests will the human make when using the system?

The next part likely to change includes the Attributes that describe items in the problem domain. Yet these changes tend to apply to a single Class, for example, "Aircraft" and its Attributes.

The most stable aspects are the Classes that strictly depict the problem domain and the system's responsibilities within that domain. For example, whether one specifies a very low budget or a very sophisticated air traffic control system, one will still have the same basic Classes with which to organize the analysis and ultimately the specification: "Aircraft," "Controller," "Airspace," etc. A more expensive system will have more Attributes for certain Classes, and will have more elaborate interfaces for monitoring devices and other systems (and additional Classes to model this). The more expensive system will have more sophisticated Services defined for each Class (e.g., "Aircraft" with an automated tracking Service, "Aircraft.Track"). Also, the more expensive version may have some additional Classes (e.g., "Radar" with corresponding Attributes, plus Services such as "Radar.Interrogate"). Yet by and large, the very stable aspect of the system (Classes in the problem domain) will remain the same across what potentially could be major changes in scope of a system's responsibilities.

And so, the designer expects and plans for change and accepts change as a fact of life, rather than condemns it as a product of sloppy thinking [derived from Fischer, 1989].

1.5 MOTIVATIONS AND BENEFITS OF OOD

The motivations and benefits of OOD are as follows:

1. *Tackle more challenging problem domains.* OOA brings extra emphasis to the understanding of problem domains. OOD and OOP (object-oriented programming) preserve the problem domain semantics.

2. *Improve problem domain expert, analyst, designer, and programmer interaction.* OOD organizes designs using the methods of organization that pervade people's thinking.

3. *Increase the internal consistency across analysis, design, and programming.* OOD reduces the bandwidth between different activities, by treating Attributes and Services as an intrinsic whole.

4. *Explicitly represent commonality.* OOD uses inheritance to identify and capitalize on commonality of Attributes and Services.

5. *Build systems resilient to change.* OOD packages volatility within problem-domain constructs, providing stability over changing requirements and similar systems.

6. *Reuse OOA, OOD, and OOP results*—accommodating both families of systems and practical tradeoffs within a system. OOD organizes results based upon problem domain and implementation domain constructs, for reuse and for subsequent reuse.

7. *Provide a consistent underlying representation* for OOA (what is to be built), OOD (how it is to be built this time), and OOP. OOD supports a continuum of representation, for systematically expanding OOA results into OOD and OOP.

Developing the Multilayer, Multicomponent Model

Webster's defines *model* as follows:

> Model. A model is a form of something to be made; a plan; a pattern.
> [*Webster's*, 1977; derived]

Designers need to conceptualize, communicate, and evaluate designs. A model provides a medium for doing so.

In OOA, the whole-part principle (presented in the previous chapter) is applied to describe its five layers:

> Subject layer
> Class-&-Object layer
> Structure layer
> Attribute layer
> Service layer

In OOD, the whole-part principle is applied to describe its four major components:

> Problem Domain Component
> Human Interaction Component
> Task Management Component
> Data Management Component

This chapter presents:

> Discovering a model
> A continuum of representation
> Five layers, five activities
> Four components, four activities
> Definitions and notation

2.1 DISCOVERING A MODEL

As method developers, the authors needed to know what components are essential to effective object-oriented design.

The approach: study effective object-oriented designers, their designs, and their code.

These designers included S. Sridahr (C++, Smalltalk, CLOS), Steve Burbeck (Object Pascal, Smalltalk, MacApp), Ken Auer (lower-level OOD, Smalltalk), Sam Adams (Smalltalk), and Jeff McKenna (Smalltalk).

Sam Adams's academic training was in chemistry, but his professional experience and expertise is in Smalltalk. He approaches OOD with a strong emphasis on simulating real-world systems. The shape of his OODs remind the authors of what one might see when using one of a number of simulation languages.

Jeff McKenna's background is programming, with some real-time system experience. He approaches OOD with a strong emphasis on modeling system responsibilities. The shapes of his designs tend to be spartan at first; he adds additional structure as things gradually become a bit too intertwined.

The authors especially studied Jeff's work during the development of OOA*Tool*™, an automated support tool for OOA. Jeff started the project and developed the domain-based Classes. Object International, Inc., signed Jeff up to develop a series of tools.

Jeff and the authors met in Austin, Texas, for a high-speed, two-day code walk-through of OOA*Tool*™, looking specifically for a model or pattern that could be used to communicate effective OOD. Late on the second day, in the midst of exhaustion, one of the authors scribbled up on the chalkboard:

Five layers, four components

...five layers

...four components

> Problem Domain Component
> Human Interaction Component
> Task Management Component
> Data Management Component

Although too tired at the moment to sense the thrill of discovery, the authors knew that the "aha!" idea had come—a pattern that happens again and again with successful object-oriented designs and implementations. A systematic approach to OOD was finally within reach.

2.2 A CONTINUUM OF REPRESENTATION

2.2.1 The Problem

Since the late 1970s, software developers have faced two "Grand Canyons" [Norman, 1990]. The first chasm is between data flow diagrams (DFDs) and entity-relationship diagrams (ERDs):

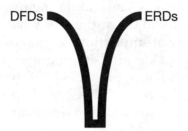

DFDs ⟍   ⟋ ERDs

Figure 2.1:   The traditional chasm between DFDs and ERDs

DeMarco noted in 1978 that DFDs weren't strong enough for data held over time. His solution at that time: a second diagram, called a data structure diagram (also called an entity-relationship diagram or ERD) [DeMarco, 1978]. An alternate solution would have been to invent a single representation that gives proper emphasis to data and the processing on that data.

The second chasm is between analysis and design:

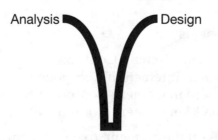

Analysis ⟍   ⟋ Design

Figure 2.2:   The traditional chasm between analysis and design

For many years, professionals have been stymied by the underlying representation shift as they moved from analysis to design. This major shift prevented designers from systematically adding design-dependent detail to the analysis results.

2.2.2 A Solution

By applying a uniform underlying representation for organizing data and its exclusive processing—that of Classes and Objects within those Classes—both chasms vanish.

OOA identifies and defines Classes and Objects that directly reflect the problem domain and the system's responsibilities within it.

OOD identifies and defines additional Classes and Objects, reflecting an implementation of the requirements. In addition, good design practice implies tradeoffs between potential approaches.

OOA and OOD consist of distinct activities—whether applied in sequence or in some intertwined fashion.

2.2.3 Some Major Implications

A uniform underlying representation scheme has a number of far-reaching implications, including:

No major difference between analysis and design notations
No "transitioning into design"
No waterfalls (unless you want one)
Yes, distinct skills and strategies
Yes, a uniform representation from OOA to OOD to OOP
    (object-oriented programming)

No major difference between analysis and design notations. One notational scheme (and its underlying representation) applies to both analysis and design. But this means that a software professional won't be able to point to the shape of a data flow bubble or a structure chart box and claim "I'm doing analysis" or "I'm doing design" (many times just the opposite was going on, anyway!), because the difference between analysis and design becomes a question of which different activities are being performed by the professional.

No "transitioning into design." For years, software professionals have been plagued with various notions, conference diagrams, and cute cartoons depicting how to yank the analysis results around into a first-cut design. In this approach, the designers go off to do the design. And they return at the end of the design, with traceability matrix in hand, to prove that they really did design to meet those fuzzy old requirements.

Yet requirements are specified to be met; and design is the careful development of a reasonable way to implement those specified requirements.

No waterfalls (unless you want one). With a uniform underlying representation for both analysis and design, the analysis does not have to be fully completed before the design begins. And that's fine, because once you recognize your lack of omniscience, you see that the probability of "fully" completing anything becomes quite remote.

With a single notational scheme, a project team can approach the development cycle as:

Waterfall—
  Analysis
  Design
  Programming

Spiral—
  Analysis, prototyping, risk management
  Design, prototyping, risk management
  Programming, prototyping, risk management
  [Boehm, 1988]

Incremental—
  A little analysis
  A little design
  A little programming
  Repeat
  [Gilb, 1988]

Nothing in OOA and OOD notations and strategies need impede any of these approaches.

These OOA and OOD may be applied in sequence. Such an approach helps with larger teams (different schedule, possibly different teams) and larger problem domains (choosing to conduct analysis at a higher level of abstraction).

OOA and OOD may be intertwined (one, then the other, again and again). In small teams, especially in a prototyping-conducive environment (e.g., Smalltalk), the activities and focus of OOA and OOD are often approached in this manner.

Yes, distinct skills and strategies. OOA and OOD activities incorporate distinct skills and strategies for effective analysis and design, respectively. OOA activities identify and define Classes and Objects that directly reflect the problem domain and the system's responsibilities within it. OOD activities identify and define additional Classes and Objects, reflecting an implementation of the requirements.

OOA results are placed directly in the Problem Domain Component. Within this component there is the potential need to manage combinations and splits of certain Classes, Structures, Attributes, and Services. Such splits are made using specific engineering criteria, and tools need to capture each decision. Criteria include reusing design and code Classes, grouping problem-domain-specific Classes together, establishing a protocol by adding a generalization Class, accommodating a supported level of inheritance, improving performance, supporting storage management, and adding lower-level detail.

The Human Interaction Component includes the actual displays and inputs needed for effective human-computer interaction. Classes will vary somewhat depending upon the graphical user interfaces (GUIs) being used, for example, Presentation Manager, Motif, MacApp, or Smalltalk. Example Classes would include project-specific (and GUI-specific) specializations of Window, Field, Graphic, and Selector.

The Task Management Component includes task (program) definition, communication, and coordination. It also includes hardware allocation considerations, plus external system and device protocols. Example Classes include TaskCoordinator and Task.

The Data Management Component includes access and management of persistent data. It isolates the data management approach, whether flat file, flat file with a tagged language, relational, object-oriented, or some other one. Example Classes include ObjectServer.

Yes, a uniform representation from OOA to OOD to OOP. Object-orientation applies a uniform underlying representation from OOA to OOD to OOP. This uniform underlying representation provides a stable framework for understandability, reusability, and extendibility.

OOA, being focused on problem domain, systems responsibilities, and requirements, is programming language-independent. Much of OOD, being focused on implementing those requirements using available technologies, still remains largely language-independent.

The programming language syntax and data management approach impact how much of the OOA and OOD *semantics* are captured explicitly in the implementation *syntax*.

For projects using less than an object-oriented programming language (OOPL), at least a uniform underlying representation is carried from the problem domain to analysis to design. The benefits are still very real. But the code itself only gets data abstraction by discipline; the syntax falls short.

Perhaps language has its most significant (and most overlooked) impact—including its ability to explicitly capture OOA and OOD semantics—after the system is delivered (where 80 percent of system dollars go! [Boehm, 1981]. With disciplined, thoughtfully prepared object-oriented programming in an OOPL, the OOA and OOD Classes are explicit in the code itself. This means that a maintainer can look at that code, perhaps in graphical form, and see the OOA and OOD Classes. From a maintainer's perspective, the ultimate documentation is the code itself; and this takes on a new significance when the code declares the OOA and OOD Classes.

2.3 FIVE LAYERS, FIVE ACTIVITIES

The OOD model, just like the OOA model, consists of five layers: Subject, Class-&-Object, Structure, Attribute, and Service.

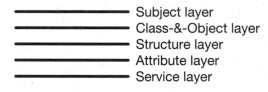

Subject layer
Class-&-Object layer
Structure layer
Attribute layer
Service layer

Figure 2.3: Five layers

These five layers are much like overlapping pieces of clear plastic (i.e., transparencies) that gradually present more and more detail. The layers are horizontal slices of the overall model.

In an overall approach, the five layers correspond to the five major activities introduced in OOA:

Finding Class-&-Objects
Identifying Structures
Identifying Subjects
Defining Attributes
Defining Services

These are indeed *activities*, not necessarily sequential steps. The activities guide one from high levels of abstraction (e.g., problem-domain Class-&-Objects) to increasingly lower levels of abstraction (Structures, Attributes, and Services). And the ordering of these five activities represents the most common *overall* approach.

At MCC (Austin, Texas), researchers have observed that analysts/designers tend to work at a high level of abstraction, then see a detailed area, dive into it, investigate it, and then return to a higher level of abstraction. In fact, we've seen the same thing with our children. And we've observed the same pattern as analysts apply OOA. Upon finding a Class-&-Object (e.g., Radar), some analysts want to add in a Service name (e.g., "I know I need SearchForAirborneItem in here."). So they write that Service name down on the Service layer and then return to continue looking for another problem domain Class-&-Object.

It is helpful as a general pattern to move from one activity to the next, but it is not mandatory. In fact, some analysts prefer to go from Class-&-Objects to Attributes to Structures to Services; others prefer to go from Class-&-Objects to Services to Structures to Attributes. This is fine; these are indeed activities. Finally, Subjects may be added, to guide readers through a larger model.

2.4 FOUR COMPONENTS, FOUR ACTIVITIES

The OOD model consists of four components:

Problem Domain Component
Human Interaction Component
Task Management Component
Data Management Component

shown graphically in the figure that follows:

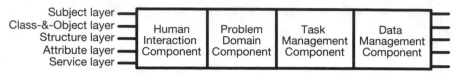

Figure 2.4: Four components

The components are vertical slices of the overall model.

In an overall approach, the four components correspond to the four major activities in OOD:

> Designing the Problem Domain Component
> Designing the Human Interaction Component
> Designing the Task Management Component
> Designing the Data Management Component

These are indeed *activities*, not sequential steps.

Chapters 3-6 present these four components, with what, why, how (strategy), and examples.

2.5 DEFINITIONS AND NOTATIONS

This section summarizes the notations for OOA and OOD:

> Class-&-Object
> Structure
> Subject
> Attribute (and Instance Connections)
> Service (and Message Connections)

The section ends with a pictorial summary of the notations.

2.5.1 Definitions and Notations—Class-&-Object

Definitions

Object. An *abstraction* of something in the domain of a problem or its implementation, reflecting the capabilities of a system to keep information about it, interact with it, or both; an *encapsulation* of Attribute values and their exclusive Services. (Synonym: an Instance.)

Class. A description of one or more Objects, describable with a uniform set of Attributes and Services; in addition, it may describe how to create new Objects in the Class.

Class-&-Object. A term meaning "a Class and the Objects in that Class."

Notations

The "Class-&-Object" symbol represents a Class and its Objects.

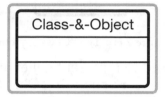

Figure 2.5: The "Class-&-Object" Symbol

The symbol represents both a Class (represented by the bold rounded rectangle divided into three horizontal sections) and its Object(s) (represented by a nonbold, lightly patterned, rounded rectangle). Certain connections map an Object to another;[1] other connections map a Class to another;[2] and other connections map an Object to a Class.[3] This notation facilitates the explicit representation of such mappings. When using paper and pencil, just a simple rounded rectangle works fine. But with CASE tool support, the Class-&-Object symbol, with its separate rounded rectangles, makes explicit whether an attached line applies to the Class or to an Object.

The symbol is labeled with its Class-&-Object name, Attribute(s) (applicable to each Object in the Class), and Service(s) (applicable to each Object in the Class).

The Class-&-Object name is a singular noun or an adjective and a noun. A Class-&-Object name should describe a single Object within the Class—for example, when each Object describes something that gets shipped, use "Shipment Item" (each Object is one item) rather than "Shipment" (which would describe an entire shipment, e.g., a truckload or plane load).

A variation on the Class-&-Object symbol is the Class symbol:[4]

---

[1] Namely, Whole-Part Structures, Instance Connections, and most Message Connections.
[2] Namely, Generalization-Specialization (Gen-Spec) Structures and certain Message Connections.
[3] Namely, certain Message Connections.
[4] Sometimes languages refer to this as an "abstract" class.

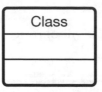

Figure 2.6: The "Class" symbol

This symbol is used to represent generalization Class from the problem domain, whose corresponding Objects are portrayed by its specializations, which have Class-&-Object symbols.

2.5.2 Definitions and Notations—Structure

Definitions

Structure. Structure is an expression of problem-domain complexity, pertinent to the system's responsibilities. The term *Structure* is used as an overall term, describing both Generalization-Specialization (Gen-Spec) Structure and Whole-Part Structure.

Generalization-Specialization (Gen-Spec) Structure may be viewed as part of the "distinguishing between Classes" aspect of the three basic methods of organization that pervade all of people's thinking. An example is the generalization Vehicle and the specialization TruckVehicle. Less formally, a Gen-Spec Structure is known as an "is a" or "is a kind of" Structure; for example, a TruckVehicle is a (is a kind of) Vehicle. Within Gen-Spec Structures, inheritance applies, with an explicit representation of more general Attributes and Services, followed by pertinent specializations.

Whole-Part Structure represents one of the three basic methods of organization that pervade all of people's thinking. An example is the whole Vehicle, and the part Engine. Less formally, a Whole-Part Structure is known as a "has a" Structure; for example, a Vehicle has an Engine.

Notations

Gen-Spec Structure. Gen-Spec Structures are shown with a Generalization Class at the top and Specialization Classes below, with lines drawn between them. The semicircle marking distinguishes Classes as forming a Gen-Spec Structure.

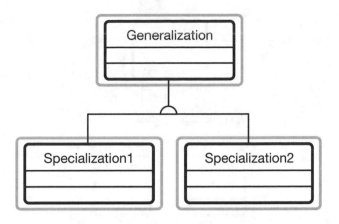

Figure 2.7: Gen-Spec Structure notation

The notation is directional; it uses a line or lines, drawn outward from the semicircle, to "point" to the generalization(s); so a Gen-Spec Structure could be drawn at any angle. However, consistently placing the generalization higher and specializations lower produces an easier-to-understand model.

The endpoints of a Gen-Spec Structure line are positioned to reflect a mapping between Classes (rather than between Objects).

Each specialization is named in such a way that it can stand on its own. An appropriate name for the specialization will typically be the name(s) of its corresponding generalization(s), accompanied by a qualifying name that describes the nature of the specialization. For example, for a generalization called Sensor, specializations "CriticalSensor" and "StandardSensor" are preferred over just merely "Critical" or "Standard."

Class-&-Object symbols appear for all bottommost specializations. At other places, either Class-&-Object or Class symbols may be appropriate.

Whole-Part Structure. Whole-Part Structure is shown with a whole Object (of a Class-&-Object symbol) at the top, and then a part Object (of a Class-&-Object symbol) below, with a line drawn between them. A triangle marking distinguishes Objects as forming a Whole-Part Structure.

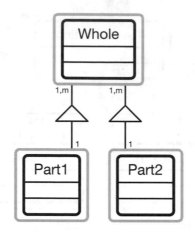

Figure 2.8:   Whole-Part Structure notation

The notation is directional, so that the Whole-Part Structure could be drawn at any angle; however, consistently placing the whole higher and parts lower produces an easier-to-understand model. This is deliberate, portraying that a whole has some number of parts. Also, note that a whole may have different kinds of parts.

The endpoints of a Whole-Part Structure line are positioned to reflect a mapping between Objects (rather than between Classes).

Each end of a Whole-Part Structure line is marked with an amount or range, indicating the number of parts that a whole may have, and vice versa, *at any given moment in time.*

2.5.3 Definition and Notations—Subject

Definition

Subject. A Subject is a mechanism for guiding a reader (analyst, problem domain expert, manager, client) through a large, complex model. (Subjects are also helpful for organizing work packages on larger projects.) Subjects are strictly a means to an end— they give an overview of a larger OOD model.

Notations

Subjects can be shown either in a "collapsed" form, a partially expanded form, or a fully expanded form, as shown on page 31.

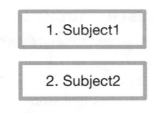

Figure 2.9: Subject notation, collapsed

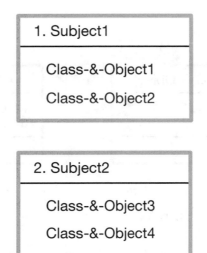

Figure 2.10: Subject notation, partially expanded (a CASE tool option)

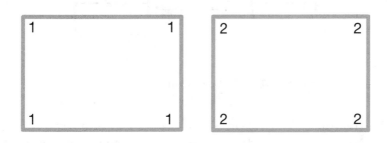

Figure 2.11: Subject notation, expanded (when shown with other layers)

2.5.4 Notation—Attribute (and Instance Connection)

Definitions

Attribute. An Attribute is some data (state information) for which each Object in a Class has its own value.

Instance Connection. An Instance Connection is a model of problem domain mapping(s) that one Object needs with other Objects, in order to fulfill its responsibilities. An Instance Connection represents part of the state information needed by an Object.

Notations

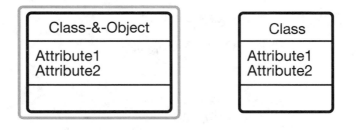

Figure 2.12: Attribute notation

Attributes are placed in the center section of the Class-&-Object and Class symbols.

Figure 2.13: Instance Connection notation

An Instance Connection is shown with a line drawn between Objects. Note that the endpoints of an Instance Connection line are positioned to reflect mappings between individual Objects (rather than between Classes).

Each Object has amount (m) or range markings (m,n) on each of its Instance Connections, reflecting its constraints with other Objects. Observe that an amount (m) or range (m,n) is being used, rather than ratios. This shows the number or range of mappings that may occur.

Explicit lower and upper bounds may be directly shown, for example, "1,5." And if a fixed number of connections must occur, then a single amount can be used (e.g., "1," when one and only one connection is required).

2.5.5 Notation—Service (and Message Connection)

Definitions

Service. A Service is a specific behavior that an Object is responsible for exhibiting.

Message Connection. A Message Connection models the processing dependency of an Object, indicating a need for Services in order to fulfill its responsibilities.

Notations

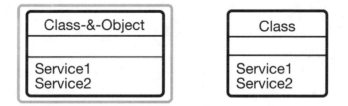

Figure 2.14:   Service notation

Services are placed in the bottom section of the Class-&-Object and Class symbols.

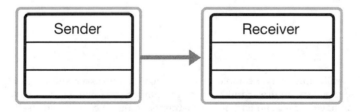

Figure 2.15:   Message Connection notation

The notation for a Message Connection is a dashed or patterned arrow. The arrow points from sender to receiver. The arrow indicates the sender "sends" a message; the receiver "receives" the message; the receiver takes some action and returns a result to the sender.[5] Each end of the arrow usually connects to an Object (or occasionally to a Class, to create a new Object), to indicate the actual participants.

2.5.6 Notation—Summary

The OOD notation is summarized by the figure on page 35:

---

[5] Generally, the receiver completes the action, *then* returns a result. Yet it's possible in OOD for the receiver to return a result, and then continue to take ongoing action. Also in OOD, a Service can have trigger and terminate constraints, so that it can activate itself without the need for a message to be sent to it.

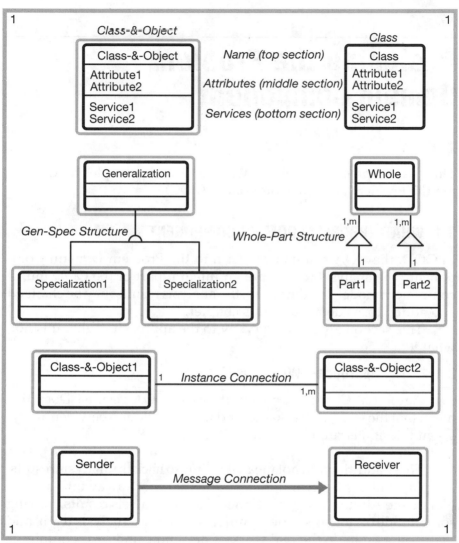

Figure 2.16: Notation summary

3

Designing the Problem Domain Component

This chapter presents the what, why, how, and examples for designing the Problem Domain Component (PDC).

3.1 WHAT—PROBLEM DOMAIN COMPONENT

In OOD, the OOA results fit right into the Problem Domain Component. The analysis results are an integral part of the OOD multi-component model. Furthermore, the analysis results may be changed and added to, as detailed in this chapter.

This section gives an overview to the approach—what it is not, what it is.

3.1.1 The Approach—What It Is Not

Agghhhh! Changes and additions to OOA results! Does this mean that the wide, untrackable, and untraceable gap between analysis and design is rumbling nearby?

No!

These additions do not mean it is time to hack up analysis results, whip up a little magic, and then suddenly "poof" away into design. Nor do the additions suggest glancing at the analysis results, making some subtle or not-so-subtle comments about the analysis team, and then going off to do the real work of designing and programming!

In OOD, the OOA results fit right into the PDC. The analysis results are an integral part of the OOD multicomponent model.

3.1.2 The Approach—What It Is

Making improvements and additions within the PDC is a trading off of modification criteria versus a desire to keep the design and programming organized as much as possible like the problem domain.

OOD additions within the PDC express actual changes needed to resolve a particular design consideration. This may require a combining or a splitting up of Class-&-Objects, Structures, Attributes, and Services. Such an addition is indeed a design issue—and justifiable technically only when based upon specific, objective criteria.

3.2 WHY—PROBLEM DOMAIN COMPONENT

With an object-oriented paradigm, one is highly motivated to keep the problem domain organizational framework intact. In this way, traceability from analysis to design to programming is evident, since each is organized like the problem domain itself.

It is a matter of striving for stability. The need is for stability (versus volatility) of analysis, design, and programming organization over time. Yes, details change—an added specialization Class here, an added Attribute or Service there. Yet with overall organizational framework being problem domain based, the organization of the results will remain stable over time.

This stability is needed for the system being prepared to graciously incorporate changing requirements. Indeed, change is expected and planned for.

Such stability is an essential key to reusability of analysis, design, and programming results across a family of systems within a problem domain or similar problem domains. This stability is needed in order to better support the extendibility of a successful system over its life span (i.e., "let's add and sell another feature").

Similarly, the stability in OOA and OOD results provides a clearer basis for conducting systematic impact assessments of proposed changes. So any modification of OOA results within the PDC— if needed at all—must be scrutinized and justified.

3.3 HOW—PROBLEM DOMAIN COMPONENT

This section presents PDC design, following this strategy:

- Apply OOA
- Use OOA results—and improve them during OOD
- Use OOA results—and add to them during OOD

Examples in this and subsequent chapters come from the problem domains of motor vehicle registering, sensor monitoring, and computer-aided software engineering.

Some examples refer to Object International's OOA*Tool*™, commercial software that provides automated support for OOA. In these examples OOA itself becomes the problem domain under consideration. Actual Classes, Structures, Attributes, and Services from OOA*Tool*™ are included in these chapters.

3.3.1 Apply OOA

Notations and strategies. A method requires both notations (a representation) and strategies (how to get the job done).

OOA (as described in *Object-Oriented Analysis* [Coad and Yourdon, 1991]) and OOD (as described in this book) use the same notations. OOA is organized around five layers. OOD is organized around four components.

Appendix B presents a concise summary of OOA strategies. For a more detailed presentation, refer to *Object-Oriented Analysis,* Scecond edition [Coad and Yourdon, 1991].

In sequence or interleaved? How does one proceed in applying OOA and OOD? Waterfall? Spiral? Incremental?

With waterfall, a project includes an analysis phase, a design phase, and an implementation phase. Waterfall for the most part implies a strict sequence, although some feedback to an earlier phase is permitted on a very limited basis (primarily the correction of defects from an earlier phase).

With spiral, a project includes analysis, design, and implementation phases, with specification, prototyping, and risk management added in each phase.

Incremental development applies OOA, OOD, and OOP into a number of small steps. For each increment (for example, 5 percent of the overall system) a professional may utilize all three activities at different times.

As described in this book, OOA and OOD *will work with any of these processes.*

Moreover, with OOA and OOD, *nothing gets in the way of those who might apply OOA, OOD, and OOP in an interleaved fashion over time.*

3.3.2 Use OOA Results—and Improve Them during OOD

Put OOA results directly into the PDC.

Some modifications are likely to occur that are modifications of the requirements specified during OOA. Some changes are due to changing requirements—the client changes; the marketplace changes;

the needed sophistication of the system changes. Other changes are due to a lack of understanding by the analyst or the available problem domain experts. It happens. It's okay to admit to being a *practicing professional*.

In either case, simply change the OOA results (following all the usual change management and control requirements within your organization). Then let them be reflected automatically in the PDC. With automation support, this could be done just that way—automatically.

3.3.3 Use OOA Results—and Add to Them during OOD

The PDC addition criteria presented in this chapter include:

- Reuse design and programming Classes
- Group problem-domain-specific Classes together
- Establish a protocol by adding a generalization Class
- Accommodate the supported level of inheritance
- Improve performance
- Support the Data Management Component
- Add lower-level components
- Don't modify just to reflect team assignments
- Review and challenge the additions to OOA results

Reuse design and programming Classes. This section describes how to add an off-the-shelf Class—from in-house or outside sources—to the PDC.

This off-the-shelf Class may be written in an OOPL. Or it may be some available software written in something less than an OOPL; in this case, wrap the software inside an intentionally designed, Service-based interface.

Add the off-the-shelf Class to the PDC.

Identify (perhaps by italicizing or "greying out" or "striking out" or "coloring in") any Attributes or Services within the off-the-shelf Class that will not be used. Keep such nonuse to a minimum (refer to the OOD criteria chapter for more on such matters).

Add a Gen-Spec specialization, from the off-the-shelf Class to the problem domain Class.

Next, identify (italicize, color, grey, or strike out) the portion of the problem domain Class that is no longer needed in that Class, those

Attributes and Services now being inherited from the off-the-shelf Class.

Next, revise the structures and connections to the problem domain Class, moving them to the off-the-shelf Class as needed. (CASE tool support should keep track of these changes from the original OOA results automatically.)

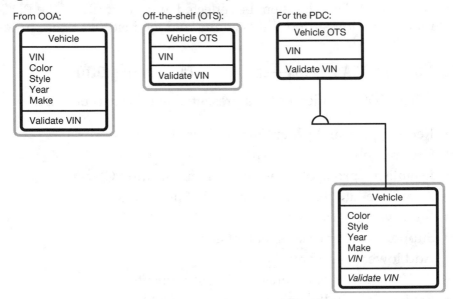

Figure 3.1: Reuse design and programming Classes

Group problem-domain-specific Classes together. Often, a Class is introduced primarily to keep problem-domain-specific Classes together.

In OOA, a Class is not introduced at the top of all the Classes, just to act as a "root" Class to group all the subordinates together. Why? It would form a Gen-Spec Structure with nearly every Class-&-Object in the OOA model—with the exception of Classes specialized elsewhere in the model. And in the tradeoff between model understandability and model semantic content, the addition of a "root" Class falls short.

Yet in OOD, a "root" Class may be introduced primarily to keep problem-domain-specific Classes together within a Class library, such as the "OOARoot" Class in the following example:

OOARoot
OOAAttribute

```
OOAClass
OOAConnection
      OOAGenSpecConnection
      OOAInstanceConnection
      OOAMessageConnection
      OOAPartConnection
OOAModelFilter
OOAModel
OOAService
OOAStrategyCard
OOASubject
```

Figure 3.2:   Group problem-domain-specific Classes together

In effect, this is a way to keep certain Classes together within a Class library, when a more sophisticated mechanism for grouping is not available. In Addition, such a Class may be put to work in establishing a protocol (discussed next).

Establish a protocol by adding a generalization Class. At times, a number of specialization Classes will need a similar protocol. What this means is that they will need to define a similar set of Services (and likely, corresponding Attributes as well). When this is the case, an additional Class may be introduced, in order to establish that proto-col—the naming of a common set of Services—to be defined in detail within specialization Classes.

For example, consider the addition of the "OOAPart" Class into the Class hierarchy:

```
OOARoot
   OOAPart
      OOAAttribute
      OOAClass
      OOAConnection
            OOAGenSpec Connection
            OOAInstanceConnection
            OOAMessageConnection
            OOAPartConnection
      OOAModelFilter
      OOAModel
      OOAService
      OOASubject
   OOAStrategyCard
```

Figure 3.3: Establish a protocol by adding a generalization Class

The OOAPart Class would not normally necessarily be needed within an OOA model. Yet it does belong in this part of the OOD model. OOAPart defines a protocol for all specializations to define and follow, for example, Services to copy, name, and describe an Object within a specialization Class.

Accommodate the supported level of inheritance. If OOA Gen-Spec Structures include multiple inheritance, some modification of OOA results will be needed when using a programming language with single or zero inheritance.

Successful systems have been built with languages that have multiple, single, and zero inheritance languages. In fact, most systems have been and continue to be built using zero inheritance languages. And while multiple inheritance languages do provide a means of more fully expressing commonality of Attributes and Services explicitly, the same basic content can be expressed in single inheritance and zero inheritance languages, too; examples follow.

Yes, a language with inheritance is desirable: it provides the syntax for capturing generalization-specialization semantics; and it provides the syntax for reusability via specialization and extension. But let's remain utterly pragmatic in an approach to design.

Multiple inheritance patterns. Consider the multiple inheritance patterns shown on page 43:

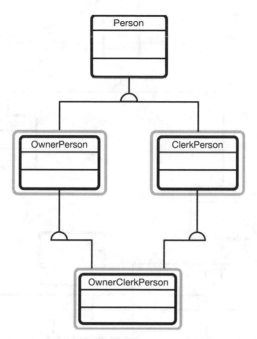

Figure 3.4:   A multiple inheritance pattern—narrow diamond

This first multiple inheritance pattern can be referred to as a narrow diamond. Attribute and Service naming conflicts come up more frequently in this pattern. And those who use it must watch out for (and have tools to help resolve) such conflicts.

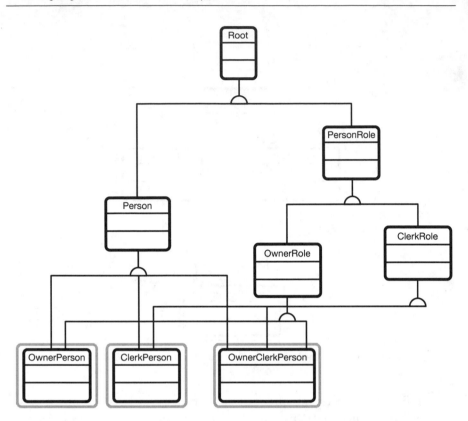

Figure 3.5: Another multiple inheritance pattern—wide diamond

This second multiple inheritance pattern can be referred to as a wide diamond; in this case, the diamond pattern starts somewhere higher than the person and role Classes: at an uppermost generalization, often referred to as a "root Class." Attribute and Service naming conflicts are less frequent here, although it requires more Classes to express the design.

Accommodating a single inheritance language. With a single inheritance language, two approaches can be applied to move from a multiple inheritance structure into a single inheritance structure.

(1) Split into multiple hierarchies, with mappings between them. In this approach, split the multiple inheritance pattern into two hierarchies, with a mapping, that is, a Whole-Part Structure or an Instance Connection, between them.

In effect, this approach models the Objects of the specialization Classes as a collection of "roles" played out by Objects of a single generalization Class.[1] For example:

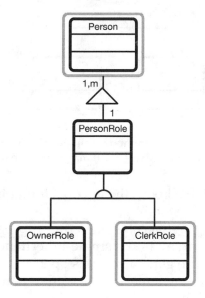

Figure 3.6:   Accommodate single inheritance—
split into separate hierarchies, with mappings between them (1)

Alternatively, this may be modeled with an Instance Connection:

---

[1] This approach is sometimes referred to as "inheritance through delegation," since the whole Object can delegate messages it does not understand to its collection of roles; it can check to see which role(s) understand(s) the message, and then it can send a message to the Service within the appropriate role(s). Multiple inheritance and inheritance through delegation provide equivalent Attributes and Services, although they are structurally different.

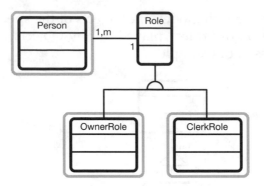

Figure 3.7: Accommodate single inheritance—
split into separate hierarchies, with mappings between them (2)

Recommendation: choose the approach that best preserves the problem domain understanding.

(2) Flatten into a single hierarchy. In this approach, flatten a multiple inheritance hierarchy into a single inheritance hierarchy. This means that one or more generalizations-specializations is no longer explicit in the design. And it means that some Attributes and Services will be repeated in the specialization Classes.

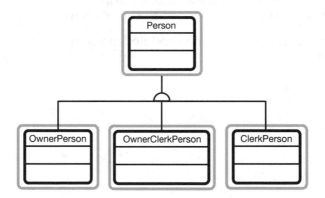

Figure 3.8: Accommodate single inheritance—
flatten into a single hierarchy

Accommodating a zero inheritance language. Inheritance in a programming language is much more than just syntactic sugar; it provides a syntax for capturing problem domain semantics, that of generalization-specialization; it explicitly expresses common Attributes and Services; and it provides a basis for reusability via extendability.

But for a variety of organizational reasons, some projects may choose to go from OOA to OOD to a zero inheritance language.

For a zero inheritance language, each Gen-Spec Structure will need to flatten the hierarchy into a grouping of Class-&-Objects—although this can be done in the programming language itself, using naming conventions to group them together, rather than explicitly in the OOD model at this point in the design.

Figure 3.9: Accommodate zero inheritance—
flatten the hierarchy into a grouping of Class-&-Objects

Improve performance. Performance, performance, performance!

Historically, performance has been a key design issue. Even with faster and faster machines, performance is still a critical factor. Yet historically, performance has meant "the faster, the better."

Or is it?

Performance. Performance is the effectiveness of the operation of something.

[*Webster's*, 1977; derived]

Performance means much more than how fast a system or an application executes. Top performing software does the right thing "fast enough" (meeting requirements or client expectation), within cost and schedule.

Improve speed. The PDC may need changes in order to improve perceived performance in the "fast enough" dimension. This happens when Objects have very high message traffic between them. Such very high coupling may indicate the need to modify the PDC by combining two or more Classes. Or by allowing a Service to surreptitiously "grab" values from another Object, bypassing the usual data abstraction principle.

But the only way to know whether such a modification will significantly contribute to making the software "fast enough" is by measuring and observing.

Measure. Modify. Measure again.

As Sam Adams put it, "fast follows function," for there is no way to effectively measure speed until some code is available to test.

Each modification of OOA results within the PDC for speed reasons must be scrutinized and justified. Modifying the PDC for speed reasons should be an absolute last resort, after all other aspects of the design are subjected to measurement and modification.

Improve perceived speed. To improve overall perceived speed, any one of the four OOD Components may add building blocks to cache some interim results.

One approach is to extend a Class-&-Object with Attributes that store interim results, for example, a month-to-date running total, whose result as of a particular date and time is held over time; subsequent calculations can take advantage of that interim result, for an improved perceived speed.

Another approach is to extend a Class-&-Object with lower-level building blocks. This forms a Whole-Part Structure. For example, in the Human Interaction Component of OOA*Tool*™, the Class OOADrawing is extended in the Human Interaction Component with some primitive display components:

> PrimitiveDisplayItem
> PrimitiveDisplayColor
> PrimitiveDisplayFont
> PrimitiveDisplayLine
> PrimitiveDisplayList
> PrimitiveDisplayPen
> PrimitiveDisplayPoints
> PrimitiveDisplayRect
> PrimitiveDisplayText

Figure 3.10:   Improve perceived speed

When a drawing element is needed, the corresponding primitives may be built up and cached in memory, until ready for display. Note that this approach encourages isolating machine dependencies within low-level Classes.

Support the Data Management Component. To support the Data Management Component, each Object to be stored needs to know how to store itself.

One approach is "each Object saves itself":

Tell an Object to save itself.

Each Object knows how to save itself.

Add an Attribute and a Service to define this.

A second approach is that each Object sends itself to the Data Management Component, which saves it:

Tell an Object to save itself.

Each Object knows what message(s) to send to the DMC, e.g., "store me," so that its state is saved. This is called a "medium-based" storage approach, where any storage system that provides the same set of Services can be plugged into the Data Management Component—without any additional modification of the Problem Domain Component.

Add Attributes, Services to define this.

For both the first and second approaches, the needed Attributes and Services are the following:

With single inheritance, modify the PDC directly.

Add an Attribute to identify an Object as belonging to a particular Class, e.g., ClassName.

Add a Service to define how an Object is to store its values.

Keep them both implicit: not included on the diagrams but defined in the text for each Class-&-Object symbol.

With multiple inheritance:

Put these additions into a new Class, then modify each PDC Class with storable Objects to include an additional generalization Class.

Put an Attribute to identify an Object as belonging to a particular Class, e.g., ClassName.

Add a Service to define how an Object is to store its values.

Keep the inheritance implicit: not on the diagrams but defined in the text for each Class-&-Object symbol.

For example, in OOA*Tool*™, each Class with storable Objects includes the Attribute "Name" and the Service "Store," which knows how to store an Object.

A third approach is: each Object to be held over time is managed by an object-oriented database management system (OO-DBMS):

Each Object is managed by an OO-DBMS and that OO-DBMS takes care of storing and retrieving Objects for the system under consideration.

An OO-DBMS provides the best potential for preserving the problem domain organizational framework throughout the design and programming. But other approaches can be reasonably managed too.

The Data Management Component itself is further detailed in a subsequent chapter.

Add lower-level components. Lower-level components may be isolated into separate Classes as a matter of convenience during design and programming. For example, in OOA*Tool*™, to factor out some of the details in low-level logic, the following Classes were added:

OOAFilterTerm
OOAFilterAND
OOAFilterLeaf
OOAFilterNOT
OOAFilterOR

Figure 3.11: Add lower-level components

Don't modify just to reflect team assignments. When making team assignments, don't split up problem-domain-based Structures or Classes. It just doesn't make sense to do so, in light of striving for stability, reusability, and extendibility. Instead, keep the PDC intact, assigning major Structures and Classes to each team.

Review and challenge the additions to OOA results. Examine the choices made. Review and challenge any OOD changes made to the contents of the PDC.

Whenever and wherever possible, preserve the problem-domain-based organization established by the OOA results.

3.3.4 Example—Sensor Monitoring System

The Sensor Monitoring System example is presented in the book *Object-Oriented Analysis* (second edition). The problem statement is expanded in this book, in order to amplify certain teaching points made in later chapters.

The Sensor Monitoring System monitors sensors and critical sensors; it also reports problem conditions.

Each sensor is described by its model (manufacturer and model number), initialization sequence (sent to the sensor to initialize it), conversion (scale factor, bias, unit of measure), sampling interval, address, state (on, off, or standby), current value, and alarm threshold.

Sensors are installed in buildings. The system keeps track of the sensors in each building, along with the building's street address and emergency contact number.

In addition, critical sensors are described by tolerance (the tolerance of the sampling interval).

The system activates certain alarm device(s) whenever a sensor threshold is met or exceeded. Alarm device activation is affected by the alarm device duration and alarm device status.

The system keeps track of the date, time, severity, time to repair, and status of each alarm.

The OOA model is shown on page 52.

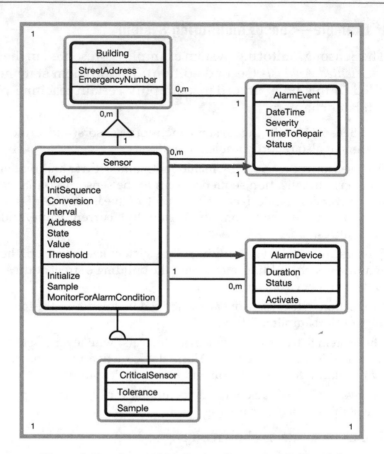

Figure 3.12: Sensor Monitoring System's OOA model

The OOA results are carried directly into the PDC within OOD. In the following figure, the Human Interaction Component (HIC), Task Management Component, and the Data Management Component are partially collapsed; the PDC (labeled as component number 1) is fully expanded.

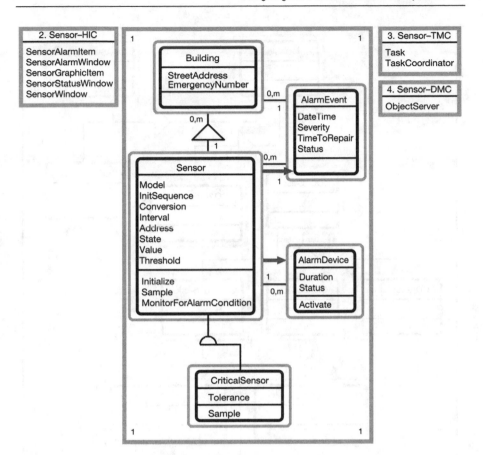

Figure 3.13: Sensor Monitoring System, PDC expanded

3.3.5 Example—OOA*Tool*™

OOA*Tool*™ is Object International's commercial software that provides automated support for OOA.

In this example, the problem domain and the system's responsibilities revolve around tooling of OOA (this is a slightly different perspective from just an OOA of OOA). Actual Classes, Structures, Attributes, and Services from OOA*Tool*™ are included in this and subsequent chapters.

The OOA model for OOA*Tool*™:

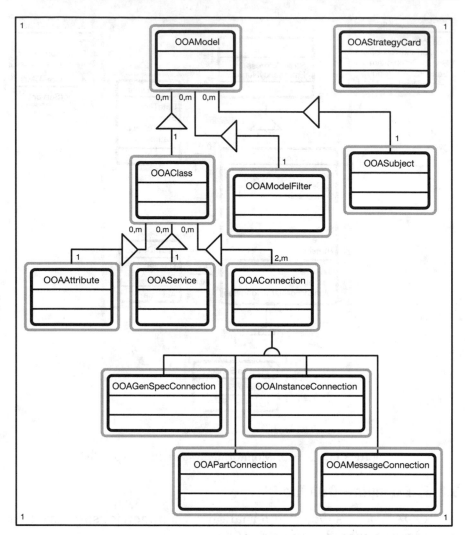

Figure 3.14: OOA*Tool*™, its OOA Model

and its corresponding Class hierarchy:

OOAAttribute
OOAClass
OOAConnection
    OOAGenSpecConnection
    OOAInstanceConnection
    OOAMessageConnection
    OOAPartConnection
OOAModel
OOAModelFilter
OOAService
OOAStrategyCard
OOASubject

Figure 3.15: OOA*Tool*™, OOA Class hierarchy

The Class hierarchy for the PDC of OOA*Tool*™ adds several Classes to the OOA results:

OOARoot
    OOAFilterTerm
        OOAFilterAND
        OOAFilterLeaf
        OOAFilterNOT
        OOAFilterOR
    OOAPart
        OOAAttribute
        OOAClass
        OOAConnection
            OOAGenSpecConnection
            OOAInstanceConnection
            OOAMessageConnection
            OOAPartConnection
        OOAModel
        OOAModelFilter
        OOAService
        OOASubject
    OOAStrategyCard

Figure 3.16: OOA*Tool*™, PDC Class hierarchy

which reflects the following PDC additions to OOA results:

OOARoot, OOAPart—added to keep a hierarchy of problem-domain-specific Classes together and to define a protocol; and

OOAFilterTerm and its specializations—added to implement the lower-level components for the logic-based combinations of model filters.

4

Designing the Human Interaction Component

This chapter presents the what, why, how, and examples for designing the Human Interaction Component (HIC).

4.1 WHAT—HUMAN INTERACTION COMPONENT

Human interaction needs detailed examination, in analysis and design.

In OOA, this detailed examination is done so that the required Attributes and Services—the required content—is specified. Prototyping is used to help during the requirements elicitation and specification, moving the requirements to being descriptive rather than just prescriptive.

In OOD, the HIC adds to those results human interaction design and the details of the interaction. This includes the designed format of windows and reports. Prototyping is used to help in the development and selection of the actual interaction mechanisms.

Some organizations may find it helpful—even essential—to design some portion of the HIC in parallel with OOA. And this is fine. Using the multilayer, multicomponent model helps to separate the implementation-dependent HIC from the OOA analysis and requirements effort; and this separation reduces the impact of change due to changes in the construction technology used to implement the human interaction itself.

Applying a systematic strategy supported by prototyping is vital to success in this area.

4.2 WHY—HUMAN INTERACTION COMPONENT

This component captures how a human will command the system and how the system will present information to the user.

Design decisions affect people. An individual's emotions and mental perceptions may be positively or negatively affected. And organizational behavior (i.e., corporate culture) may change, too. The affect can be wide reaching, spanning many responses:

- Fright, anger, exasperation, awkwardness
- Boredom
- Creativity, exhilaration

Analysts study people in order to get the context and content right during OOA. Designers need to continue to study people, this time designing the interaction specifics, using the interaction technologies available for a particular system.

4.3 HOW—HUMAN INTERACTION COMPONENT

The strategy to design this component consists of the following:

- Classify the humans
- Describe the humans and their task scenarios
- Design the command hierarchy
- Design the detailed interaction
- Continue to prototype
- Design the HIC Classes
- Design, accounting for Graphical User Interfaces (when applicable)

The sequence of these activities reflects a healthy set of priorities in human interaction design: the human, then the task, then the tool.

Human factors comprise an entire discipline unto itself, worthy of careful study and additional consideration. Consider consulting a human interaction specialist and conducting human factors testing. For further reading, refer to Laurel [1990], Norman, [1988], Rubin [1988], and Shneidermann [1987].

4.3.1 Classify the Humans

Take the time to study the humans who will use the system. As Peter's dad says, "Put yourself in someone else's shoes, and stay there for a while."

This requires some on-site time, watching the humans actually do their job; this is absolutely essential—and no contractual or sociological barriers should stand in the way of this study. Moreover, this effort requires some genuine identification with and empathy for the humans whose lives the system will affect for better or for worse. Design affects the everyday life of other humans.

Think about what these people want to accomplish. What tasks do they need to accomplish? What tools can you provide to support that task? How can the tools be made most unobtrusive?

Begin by classifying the humans into different categories. As a start in this classifying, if a "Person" Gen-Spec Structure is present in the Domain Component, use its generalization-specialization pattern as a starting point. For example, with a Registration and Title System:

> Person/Clerk/Owner/OwnerClerk

Then consider additional subsets of humans who will interact with the system under consideration. Consider classifying by one or more of the following:

> Classify by skill level
>> Novice/Occasional/Intermediate/Advanced
>
> Classify by organizational level
>> Executive/Officer/Staff
>>
>> Supervisor/Clerk
>
> Classify by membership in different groups
>> Staff/Customer

4.3.2 Describe the Humans and Their Task Scenarios

For each category of human defined in the previous step, consider and tabulate the following:

> Who
>
> Purpose
>
> Characteristics (age, level of education, limitations, etc.)
>
> Critical success factors
>> Needs/wants
>>
>> Likes/dislikes/biases
>
> Skill level
>
> Task scenarios

For each category of human, think through and write this information in the first person.

Here is an example in applying this approach, from OOA*Tool*™:

Who: I'm an analyst.

Purpose: I want to do the actual analysis work. Give me a tool that will help me be more effective (and off-load any drawing or checking drudgery that otherwise might fall my way).

Characteristics:

Age: I'm 42 years old.

Level of education: I'm a college grad.

Limitations: I don't like fine print; anything less than 9 points is just too small.

Critical success factors:

I want to do the analysis work. The tool must keep out of the way of my doing effective analysis.

Give me shortcuts so that the tool does not interfere with the work I'm doing. Make it fun.

I want the tool to capture assumptions, ideas, and trade-offs in real time.

I want to document any part of the model at any moment. I think that this information is just as important as the requirements themselves.

Skill Level: My skill level is advanced.

Task scenarios

Main scenario:

I identify the "core" Class-&-Objects.

I then identify the "core" Structures.

All along, as I find Attributes and Services, I add those that come to mind. But I don't want to see them on the model until later in my work.

I check the model.

I print the model and its full documentation.

Here is another example in applying this approach, from OOA*Tool*™:

Who: I'm an executive.

Purpose: I want to use analysis results to understand my business and to help me reshape my business for strategic advantage.

Characteristics

Age: I'm 52 years old.

Level of education: I'm a college grad.

Limitations: I don't like fine print; anything less than 10 points is just too small.

Critical success factors:

I want to see only those items that matter to me (and not a bit more).

Use my terminology or forget it.

Task scenarios

Main scenario:

My staff prepares a model for me, filtering out what they think is extraneous detail.

I look at the model and tell them what I really need.

I move around the symbols on the model, looking for strategic advantages through new combinations of data and calculations on that data.

4.3.3 Design the Command Hierarchy

It's time now for designing the command hierarchy. Include the following:

- Study the existing user interaction metaphors and guidelines
- Establish an initial command hierarchy
- Refine the command hierarchy

Study the existing human interaction metaphors and guidelines. If the command hierarchy is to exist within an established interaction system, begin by studying the existing human interaction metaphors and guidelines. This is especially true for graphical user interfaces.

Such guidelines may be informal (e.g., "it looks and feels like this"). Or they may be formally stated, such as Apple Computer's rather extensive guidelines for the Macintosh [Apple, 1988]. In either case, human interaction metaphors and guidelines evolve over time. So continue to look for, study, prototype, and incorporate good examples (later in this chapter, the prototyping aspect is further explored).

Establish an initial command hierarchy. A command hierarchy may be presented to humans in a number of ways:

- A series of menu screens
- A menu bar
- A series of icons that take actions when something is dropped on them

An astute seminar participant pointed out to us that a command hierarchy is a presentation of available Services, organized using *procedural abstraction*. Indeed, at this point the design moves to the presentation organization of the required Services, using procedural abstraction.

Begin with this basic procedural abstraction of Services and modify it to suit your specific needs:

File Edit Format Calculate Monitor Window

Figure 4.1: Initial Menu Bar

Refine the command hierarchy. To refine the hierarchy, consider ordering, whole-part chunking, breadth versus depth, and minimal steps.

Ordering. As you develop such a hierarchy, carefully select distinct Service names. And order the Service names within each part of the hierarchy: (1) with the most frequently used Service appearing first in the list, and (2) in customary work-step order.

Whole-part chunking. Look for whole-part patterns across the Services themselves, to help in organizing and chunking Services within the hierarchy.

Breadth and depth chunking. Work within the guidelines of keeping from overloading a human's short-term memory limitations. Dr. Miller, in "The Magical Number Seven, Plus or Minus Two: Some Limits on Our Capacity for Processing Information" [Miller, 1956], reported that human short-term memory seems to be limited to about five to nine items at a time. (Unless a person has been taught to use linked-list memory tricks.) Miller added to this work in 1975, with the paper "The Magic Number Seven after Fifteen Years" [Miller, 1975]. In that paper, Miller reconsiders the matter, saying that rather than seven plus or minus two, it's better viewed as three "chunks" of up to three items each.

To apply Dr. Miller's work, watch the depth versus breadth of the command hierarchy. Strive for a breadth of about three chunks of three. Limit the depth to about three—so the human doesn't have to keep a complex mental model of how far down into the application he or she may have wandered.

Minimal Steps. Minimize the number of clicks, drags, and key combinations to get the job done for the human. Provide shortcuts for advanced users of the system.

Example: OOATool.™ Beginning with the initial template, and applying the principles of ordering, breadth versus depth, and chunking, the basic menu is expanded (in this example, for the Macintosh) to the following:

File
  New Drawing
  Open Drawing...
  Open Item

  Close
  Save Drawing
  Save Drawing as...
  Revert to Saved

  Page Setup...
  Print...

  Quit

Edit
  Undo

  Cut
  Copy
  Paste
  Clear

  Select All
  Find...

  Change

Drawing
  Select Filter
  Document
  Overview

  Subject Layer
  Structure Layer
  Attribute Layer
  Service Layer

Create
  New Class
  New Subject
  New Annotation

  New Attribute
  New Service

  Change to Class-&-
      Object/Class
  Make Part Of...
  Instance Connection...
  Message Connection...
Modify
  Hide
  Restore Hidden...
  Expand
  Collapse

  Switch Sides
  Move To Top

Font
  Classes Title...
  Classes Bodies...
  Subjects Title...
  Subjects Bodies...
  Subjects Number...
  Connections...
  Annotations...

  Class Title...
  Class Body...
  Subject Title...
  Subject Body...
  Subject Number...
  Connection...
  Annotation...

Window
  Send To Back
  Collapse
  Zoom

  Redraw Screen
  Stack Windows

  Model Control
  Model Critique
  Model Template

  Strategy Cards

Figure 4.2: OOA*Tool*™, an expanded menu

4.3.4 Design the Detailed Interaction

Human interaction can be designed (and later assessed) based upon a number of criteria, including:

Consistency. Use consistent terms, consistent steps, and consistent actions.

Few steps. Minimize the number of keystrokes or mouse clicks and even the pull-down menu distance needed in order to get something done. Minimize the time needed to get meaningful results by different skill levels—novice, occasional, and advanced.

No "dead air." "Dead air" is a broadcasting term, used to describe air time without sound. Here, no "dead air" means that a human should not be left alone, without any feedback on (1) that progress is being made and (2) how much progress is being made, whenever the human must wait for a system to complete one of its actions. All of this means that meaningful, timely feedback is a must.

Closure. Use small steps, leading to a well-defined action. The human should feel a sense of closure in his or her actions.

Undo. Humans make mistakes. And humans are used to undoing—at least some of them (and it would be nice to have the option to undo any of them). The same goes for actions taken within human interaction with an automated system. If the rate of undo's for a particular action is high, then that part of the interaction should be revisited and refined.

No memory storage in "human RAM." The human should not have to remember or write down information from one window, to then be applied in another window. Program the computer, not the person. In addition, whatever the human needs to remember in the way of special key sequences and the like should be organized for ease of recall.

Time and effort to learn. Keep it short. Don't expect people to read printed documentation, let alone study it in detail for its subtleties and nuances. Provide an on-line reference for more advanced features (so humans can discover them as they find a need for them).

Pleasure and appeal (look and feel). Humans use software that is fun to use. Humans will tolerate other software, but only if and while they must.

For look, apply graphic design principles [Berryman, 1984]. For feel, prototype and watch the human. There is more on this in the following section.

4.3.5 Continue to Prototype

Prototyping begins in OOA and continues now in OOD.

Prototyping the human-computer interaction is essential for the HIC design. Humans need to experience, play with, and refine the proposed interaction into a consistent pattern. The interface should be nonobtrusive; that is, the human spends minimum time thinking about the mechanics of using the interface and maximum time doing the work he or she is actually trying to get done.

Even better is an interface that actually enhances the human's performance. Yet "look and feel" is not well understood. A good place to start is with some existing software with a well-respected human interface. If one can be found within the problem domain you are dealing with, so much the better.

Consider menus, pop-ups, fill-ins, and command shortcuts. Use a visual prototyping tool or small application builder; these keep getting better and better (e.g., Prograph™ on the Macintosh). Prototype several alternatives. Then let humans try each one out. Don't fall into the trap of watching your nifty new interface. Instead, watch the person! Watch the reaction of various humans who use the interface. Gradually iterate toward a more and more effective interface.

In Japanese product development, a new concept in quality is much more than just the absence of defects. The new concept is called *miroyokutaki hinshitsu*, meaning "things gone right," with the connotation of something fascinating, enticing, and delightful. It's more than "look and feel." It's subliminal quality leading to strong emotional satisfaction. And such satisfaction comes from the fine tuning of each piece of the human interaction to be the best it can be. To apply this concept, ask questions like:

How do you feel at this point?
What is it that you really would like next?
What command sequence just plain gets in your way?
What help do you need to do a more effective job at this point?

Some product developers videotape the person, under the pretext of wanting to record the person's comments. Yet when they review the tape, they find that watching the person's facial expressions and body language may reveal much more about whether or not *miroyokutaki hinshitsu* is being achieved.

Perhaps heart and breathing rates would also be interesting considerations.

So, it's more than just "look and feel." It's emotional satisfaction, derived from the fine tuning of each piece of human interaction to its appeal-factor potential.

4.3.6 Design the HIC Classes

HIC Classes will vary somewhat depending upon the graphical user interface being used, such as Presentation Manager, Motif, MacApp, or Smalltalk. (Additional, specific graphical user interface design considerations are addressed later in this chapter.)

To design the HIC Classes, begin by organizing the human interaction design by windows and components:

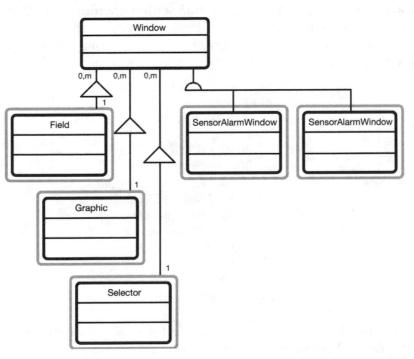

Figure 4.3:   Windows and components

This pattern can be specialized further. For example, in OOA*Tool*.™

```
OOARoot
  OOAWindow
    OOAClassWindow
    OOAConditionWindow
    OOACritiqueWindow
    OOADocumentWindow
    OOADrawingWindow
    OOAFilterWindow
    OOAModelControlWindow
    OOAStrategyWindow
    OOATemplateWindow
```

Each Class contains the definition of the menu bar, pull-down menu, and pop-up menus for a window. Each Class also defines the Services needed to create the menus, highlight a selected item, and invoke the corresponding response. Each Class is also responsible for the actual presentation of information within a window. Moreover, each Class encapsulates all of its physical dialogue considerations.

Add Classes for drawing graphic icons within a window when such a capability is needed. For example:

```
OOARoot
  OOADrawing
    OOADrawingItem
  OOAGraphic
    OOAClassNode
    OOAGraphicConnection
      OOAAttributeConnection
      OOAGenSpecConnection
      OOAMessageConnection
      OOAPartConnection
    OOATextNode
  OOALine
    OOACorner
  OOASmartLine
```

Similarly, add Classes for selecting items within windows, when such a capability is needed. For example:

```
OOARoot
  OOASelector
    OOAConnectionSelector
    OOANilSelector
    OOANodeSelector
    OOANodesSelector
    OOASubjectSelector
```

Selectors contain selected item(s). Selectors cache mouse clicks, to distinguish between a single click and a double click. Selectors detect mouse button hold-downs. The selectors take corresponding action, including graphical user feedback based upon where the cursor is.

Add a Class for font control. For example:

```
OOARoot
  OOAFont
```

Add Classes to support cut and paste. For example:

```
OOARoot
  OOAPasteHolder
  OOAPaster
```

The machine dependencies of the human-computer interaction may be encapsulated within these identified Classes or their specialization Classes (to even further isolate machine dependencies).

4.3.7 Design, Accounting for Graphical User Interfaces

This section presents the core aspects of graphical user interface (GUI, pronounced "gooey") technology, applicable if and when a GUI is needed within a particular design.

Leading GUIs include Macintosh, Windows, Presentation Manager, X Windows, and Motif. And for a subset of GUI commands, the concepts can be mapped even down to character mode terminals. With GUIs, look and feel is platform-specific. Careful study of the best-selling applications on a platform—for the strong points and the annoyances, too—is essential for meeting expectations of more demanding humans.

GUIs have key differences, for example, typefaces, coordinate systems, and events. For GUI *typefaces*, font/size/style may be limited to certain combinations or may be available in any combination. For GUI *coordinate systems,* the origin (upper left or lower left), the supported display resolution, and the supported display dimensions vary. GUI *events* lie at the core of GUI code. Services respond to events, whether from a human or from some other Service.

GUI events work in two ways: direct or queued (or, at times, with a combination of these two).

Direct. An event occurs, and the system itself executes the corresponding event-handler routine previously registered by an application program. In this case, a single item in a window may have its own event handler, directly executed when an event occurs.

Queued. An event occurs and is queued by the system. Each event may be tagged with some routing information. Applications call "next event" to get an event and then take whatever action is needed.

Can a GUI toolkit be designed to straddle the different GUIs? Perhaps. Some commercial toolkits do so, but they sacrifice some of the platform-specific look-and-feel characteristics. Some OOPL class libraries do a better job of this (e.g., Digitalk's Smalltalk/V). And it seems reasonable that one could develop a nearly portable GUI toolkit, without suppressing all platform-specific nuances, by:

> Developing a command set that is a superset of the target command sets

> Using a consistent event model—direct, with an extra set of routines to provide the event queue model, when needed

> Supplying and registering GUI-specific event handlers within the nearly portable GUI software

> [Nicholson, 1991]

As an example, consider OOA*Tool*™. The GUI code was isolated to specific Services in order to minimize machine dependencies. By using this approach, and the Smalltalk/V class library, the lead developer moved the application from Macintosh to Windows in several weeks, and from Windows to OS/2 in several days.

4.3.8 Example—Sensor Monitoring System

Approach:

> Classify the humans. Hi. I'm Fred. I want to be in control of my sensors. I want to add them, initialize them, and then control their operation, switching between on, standby, and off, as I see fit.

Define the task scenarios. I want to add a sensor —> I want to initialize a sensor —> I want to turn the sensor on —> the system reports an alarm condition (red flasher and a volume-adjustable buzzer, min. volume 20 db) —> I go out and correct the problem.

Design the command hierarchy.

File	Edit	Initialize	State	Style
	Add...		Off	Font...
	Change...		Standby	Icon size...
	Delete...		On	

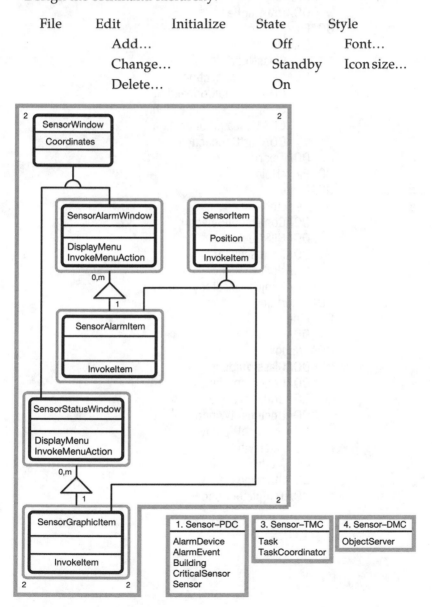

Figure 4.4: Sensor Monitoring System, HIC expanded

4.3.9 Example—OOA*Tool*™

The HIC in OOA*Tool*™:

```
OOARoot
    OOADrawing
        OOADrawingItem
    OOAFont
    OOAGraphic
        OOAClassNode
        OOAGraphicConnection
                OOAAttributeConnection
                OOAGenSpecConnection
                OOAMessageConnection
                OOAPartConnection
        OOATextNode
    OOAPasteHolder
    OOAPaster
    OOASelector
        OOAConnectionSelector
        OOANilSelector
        OOANodeSelector
        OOANodesSelector
        OOASubjectSelector
    OOASmartLine
    OOALine
        OOACorner
    OOAWindow
        OOAClassWindow
        OOAConditionWindow
        OOACritiqueWindow
        OOADocumentWindow
        OOADrawingWindow
        OOAFilterWindow
        OOAModelControlWindow
        OOAStrategyWindow
        OOATemplateWindow
```

```
PrimitiveDisplayItem
     PrimitiveDisplayColor
     PrimitiveDisplayFont
     PrimitiveDisplayLine
     PrimitiveDisplayList
     PrimitiveDisplayPen
     PrimitiveDisplayPoint
     PrimitiveDisplayRect
     PrimitiveDisplayText
OOADocumentItem
     OOADocumentClassItem
     OOADocumentDrawingItem
     OOADocumentFilterItem
     OOADocumentHolderItem
     OOADocumentModelItem
     OOADocumentTopItem
```

Figure 4.5: OOA*Tool*™, HIC Class hierarchy

5

Designing the Task Management Component

This chapter presents the what, why, how, and examples for designing the Task Management Component (TMC).

5.1 WHAT—TASK MANAGEMENT COMPONENT

A task is defined as:

> Task. Another name for a process (a stream of activity, defined by its code). The concurrent execution of a number of tasks is referred to as multitasking.
>
> [*Oxford*, 1986]

For certain kinds of systems, multiple tasks are required:

For systems with data acquisition and control responsibility for local device(s), multiple tasks are needed.

For certain human interfaces—ones in which multiple windows may be simultaneously selected for input—multiple tasks are also needed.

For multi-user systems, multiple copies of a user task(s) are likely.

For multisubsystem software architectures, task(s) may be used to coordinate and communicate between the pieces.

For multiple tasks on a single processor, a task may be needed to coordinate and communicate with other tasks during their execution. Together with an operating system, such tasks run in a time-sliced fashion, producing an illusion that the tasks are running at the same time.

For multiprocessor hardware architectures, separate task(s) are needed for each processor, plus tasks to support the interprocessor communication.

For a system responsible to communicate with another system, multiple tasks are needed.

Yet tasks add complexity during designing, coding, and ongoing engineering. So each one must be carefully selected and ultimately justified.

5.2 WHY—TASK MANAGEMENT COMPONENT

For certain applications, tasks simplify the overall design and code.

Separate tasks separate behaviors that must go on concurrently. This concurrent behavior may be implemented on separate processors or may be simulated when a single processor is used in conjunction with a multitasking operating system.

The alternative? A reasonable approach to consider is a cyclic executive sequential program; it executes small, fast program chunks; after each chunk, it checks to see what happened while it was busy and responds accordingly.

A far less desirable approach would be to interweave concurrent behaviors into one sequentially executed program. And this could be done. But the design and code become unwieldy in a hurry. Consider the complexity of the resulting program. It would be written as one large program. But it would be sprinkled with tests every couple of lines of source code. Each test would need to look for incoming data or request and jump off to do that work, all the while looking for yet another (perhaps higher-priority) input or request. The result: spaghetti code!

Why tasking: simplify the design and code of needed concurrent behavior. Why not tasking: avoid adding concurrent behavior just because you can; such a practice adds complexity in design, code, test, and maintenance.

Task selection and definition is presented in the section that follows.

5.3 HOW—TASK MANAGEMENT COMPONENT

This section presents task selection and justification, following this strategy:

- Identify event-driven tasks
- Identify clock-driven tasks
- Identify priority tasks and critical tasks
- Identify a coordinator
- Challenge each task
- Define each task

The point of this strategy is to identify and design the tasks plus the Services included in each task.

This strategy section builds upon and extends the tasking ideas developed by Hassan Gomaa [Gomaa, 1989].

5.3.1 Identify Event-Driven Tasks

Certain tasks are event-driven. Such tasks may be responsible for communication with a device, one or more windows on a screen, another task, a subsystem, another processor, or another system.

A task may be designed to trigger upon an event, often signaling the arrival of some data. That data may come from an input data line or it may come from a data buffer, written into by another task.

Here is how such a task works when a system is running: the task sleeps (not consuming processing time), waiting for an interrupt from a data line or some other source; upon receipt of the interrupt, the task wakes up, gobbles up the data, puts it in a buffer in memory or some other destination, notifies whoever needs to know about it, and then goes back to sleep.

5.3.2 Identify Clock-Driven Tasks

These tasks are triggered to do some processing at a specified time interval. Certain devices may need periodic data acquisition and control. Certain human interfaces, subsystems, tasks, processors, or other systems may need periodic communication. And this is often what a clock-driven task is used for.

Here's how such a task works when a system is running. The task sets a wake-up time and goes to sleep. The task sleeps (not consuming processing time), waiting for an interrupt from the system. Upon receipt of that interrupt, the task wakes up, does its work, notifies whoever needs to know about it, and then goes back to sleep.

5.3.3 Identify Priority Tasks and Critical Tasks

A priority task accommodates either high-priority or low-priority processing needs. A critical task is used to isolate processing that is especially critical to the success or failure of the system under consideration, processing that often has especially stringent reliability constraints.

High priority. Some Services may be very high priority. Such Service(s) may need to be isolated into a separated task in order to get the Service accomplished within an urgent time constraint. Additional task(s) may be used to isolate such processing.

Low priority. At the other end of the spectrum, some Services may be low priority, ones that can be relegated to lower-priority processing (often referred to as background processing). Additional task(s) may be used to isolate such processing.

High criticality. Some Services may be highly critical to the continued operation of the system under consideration. And some of those Services may be essential for continued operation even during a degraded mode of operation. Additional task(s) may be used to isolate such critical processing; this isolation partitions the intensive design, programming, and testing required for high-reliability processing.

5.3.4 Identify a Coordinator

With three or more tasks, consider adding another task. This task can act as a coordinator.

Such a task adds overhead; context switch time (the time to switch from one task to another) may discourage this design approach. Yet such a task does bring the benefit of encapsulation of intertask coordination. And its behavior is describable with a state transition matrix.

Use this kind of task to coordinate the tasks, and nothing more; do not use it to implement Services that better belong in the Class-&-Objects allocated to the tasks being coordinated.

5.3.5 Challenge Each Task

Keep the number of tasks to a minimum.

Just having one or several things going on at a time can be challenging enough in terms of understandability during both development and maintenance.

As our colleague Tom Jensen reports, the main problem in designing multiple-task systems is that designers often get enamored with tasks and define too many of them. As an example, an individual designer might add task(s) just for the sake of personal convenience in dealing with his own little piece of design and programming; yet the understandability and technical complexity of the overall design is likely to suffer.

So challenge each task. Make sure that it satisfies one or more of the engineering criteria for task selection—event-driven, clock-driven, priority/critical, or coordinating.

5.3.6 Define Each Task

Define each task by what it is, how it coordinates, and how it communicates.

What it is

Begin by specifying what the task is: name the task; describe the task briefly.

Add a new constraint—task name—to each Service in the OOD components. Assign that constraint a value for each Service in the OOD components.

If a single Service is split across more than one task, then modify the Service names and descriptions so that each Service can be mapped to one task. If such a split occurs in the PDC, an automated tool should account for and keep track of the required Service and the new Services that correspond.

For Services that include coordination and communication with devices, other tasks, or other systems, expand the Service specification with protocol-specific detail.

How it coordinates

Define how each task coordinates. Indicate whether the task is event-driven or clock-driven. For event-driven tasks, describe the event(s) that triggers it. For clock-driven tasks, describe the time interval to elapse before the task is triggered. Plus, indicate whether it is a one-time interval or a repeating one.

How it communicates

Define how each task communicates. From what does the task get its values (e.g., an input line, a mailbox, a semaphore, a buffer, or a rendezvous)? Where does the task send its values (e.g., an output line, a mailbox, a semaphore, a buffer, or a rendezvous)?

A template

The preceding paragraphs can be summarized with the following TMC template:

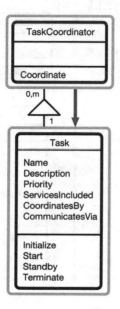

Figure 5.1: OOD notation template for the TMC

in which each task is defined with the following:

Name
Description
Priority
Services included
Coordinates by
Communicates via

Figure 5.2: OOD task definition template for the TMC

5.3.7 Example—Sensor Monitoring System

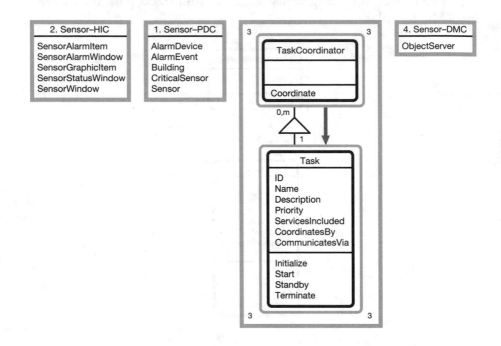

Figure 5.3: Sensor Monitoring System, TMC expanded

Task 1
>   Name: SensorReader
>   Description: This task is responsible for reading
>   sensors at the required interval
>   Services included: Sensor.Sample
>   Priority: medium
>   Coordinates by: clock-driven, at an interval of 100
>   milliseconds
>   Communicates via:
>   Gets values from an input line (from a sensor)
>   Sends values to the RawData mailbox

Task 2
>   Name: CriticalSensorReader
>   Description: This task is responsible for reading
>   critical sensors, at the required interval and
>   within the specified tolerance

Services included:
    CriticalSensor.Sample
Priority: high
Coordinates by: clock-driven, at an interval of 25
    milliseconds
Communicates via:
    Gets values from an input line (from a
        critical sensor)
    Sends values to the RawData mailbox

Task 3
    Name: InteractionCoordinator
    Description: This task is responsible for human
        interaction, sensor initialization, and
        threshold comparisons
    Services included:
        Sensor.Initialize
        Sensor.MonitorForAlarmCondition
    Priority: low
    Coordinates by: event-driven, by
        (1) human interaction event
        (2) an arrival of data event (from the RawData
            mailbox)
    Communicates via:
        Gets values from a human interaction buffer
        or from the RawData mailbox

Figure 5.4:   Sensor Monitoring System, task descriptions

5.3.8 Example—OOA*Tool*™

In OOA*Tool*™, all Services are implemented in a single task. No
TMC design is needed.

Designing the Data Management Component

This chapter presents the what, why, how, and examples for designing the Data Management Component (DMC).

6.1 WHAT—DATA MANAGEMENT COMPONENT

The Data Management Component provides the infrastructure for the storage and retrieval of objects from a data management system.

6.2 WHY—DATA MANAGEMENT COMPONENT

The Data Management Component isolates the impact of data management scheme, whether flat file, relational, object-oriented (or some other one).

6.3 HOW—DATA MANAGEMENT COMPONENT

This section presents data management approaches, assessing data management tools, and designing the Data Management Component. For additional reading in data management, refer to Parsaye, Chignell, Khoshafian, Wong, [1989], Date [1986], and others listed in the bibliography.

6.3.1 Data Management Approaches

Before the chapter marches ahead with the design impact of various data management approaches, this section describes the three major data management approaches—flat file, relational, and object-oriented.

Flat file management. Flat file management offers rudimentary file handling and sorting capabilities.

Relational database management system. Relational database management systems are built upon relational theory. This section sticks to the practical considerations of using a relational database management system (rather than strays into the somewhat theoretical world of relations, tuples, and the like).

A relational database management system manages data in some number of tables. Each table is named. Its columns are named. And each row represents one set of values within a table. Each column has a single (atomic) value in it; companion tools such as report generators rely upon this simplicity.

Tables, with name, column names, and column constraints, are defined in a database schema.

Special operations make it possible to cut and paste tables, based upon specific criteria, to make additional tables. Such operations include select (extract certain rows), project (extract certain columns), and join (pair off the rows across the tables, then extract certain rows). By using such operations, inter-row relationships do not have to be predefined (as in flat file management).

Each row must be uniquely identifiable. One or more columns may be defined as the primary key—the unique identifier for each row in a table. One or more columns may be defined as a foreign key, to facilitate accessing corresponding rows within another table.

Tables and their columns can be reorganized to reduce data redundancy and consequently reduce the number of steps needed to modify data consistently. The discipline for doing this is called normalization. The degree of data redundancy elimination is defined in "normal forms." The first normal form is the lowest level of data redundancy removal and the fifth normal form is the highest level of data redundancy removal:

First normal form
> The Attribute value must be atomic—meaning it has exactly one value and has no internal structure. This means that for each Attribute, there is no repetition of values and no internal data structure.

Second normal form
> First normal form, plus each non-key Attribute describes something identifiable only by the entire key (and not identifiable just by using part of the key).

Third normal form
> Second normal form, plus each non-key Attribute depends only on the key and is not just a further description of another non-key Attribute.

Fourth normal form
> Third normal form, plus the values of two or more non-key Attributes do not always map to another non-key Attribute.

Fifth normal form
> Fourth normal form, plus the values of two or more non-key Attributes do not always map to another non-key Attribute, following a join operation.

The price for normalization? First is the increase in the number of tables; this results in more complicated "store myself" Services. Second is the decrease in the match between the tables and problem-domain-based constructs. This results in less data management stability as the requirements change during the development of a system or a family of systems. Next in the price list is the performance (speed) cost for accessing more tables and cutting and pasting tables. This is such a critical issue that for data redundancy, "eliminate data redundancy" in practice always seems to translate into "control as much data redundancy as you can, as long as you can meet the performance requirements or expectations." Our colleague Andrew V. Zitelli has tuned relational database management systems for well over a decade; and he has yet to deliver a system in fully third normal form (let alone fourth or fifth normal form!).

Object-oriented database management system. Object-oriented database management systems are an emerging implementation technology. Commercial products first appeared in 1986. Even five years later, however, platforms are very limited and prices are relatively high. Vendors are taking one of two major approaches—extended relational and extended OOPL.

Extended relational products augment a relational database management system, adding abstract data types and inheritance, plus some general-purpose Services to create and manipulate Classes and Objects.

Extended OOPL products augment an object-oriented programming language with syntax and capability to manage remembrance of an Object over time within a database. This may give a developer a seamless view of all Objects; translating between storage data structures and program data structures is no longer needed; a fully seamless view can occur if and only if the OO-DBMS uses the *identical* Object model as its corresponding OOPL.

Most Object data management schemes today support a "copied

Objects" approach: saving the values of an Object, and then later creating a copy of that Object. An extended OOPL OO-DBMS may do more than this, providing a "persistent Objects" approach: one that saves exactly the same object, including its internal identifier, rather than just a copy of the Object. In this way, when an Object is retrieved from storage, it is identical to the Object that existed previously. The "persistent Object" approach provides a basis for shared access to a single Object from an Object server within a multi-user environment.

6.3.2 Assessing Data Management Tools

Data management tools can be assessed across a number of criteria, summarized by the following:

Underlying model—flat file,
   relational, object-oriented,
   or other
Data definition and
   manipulation language
Attribute Constraints
   Domain constraints
   Reference (Whole-Part, Instance
   Connection) constraints
     Range, value
     Support (if any) for
     reciprocal references
   Multi-Attribute constraints
   Service-described constraints
   Value-based Service triggers
Transaction management
   Protocol
   Pessimistic, optimistic
Concurrency
   Locks
   Lock granularity (Object,
     Collection, Class)
Distributed management
   Client-server architecture
   Fragmentation vs. replication control
   Transparency
     Of location

Of noncritical site or
   communication failure
Access & authorization granularity (e.g.,
   Attribute, Service, Object, Collection,
   Class)
Storage management
   Clustering
   Buffering
   Indexing
   Query optimization
     (reordering, buffering)
   Physical access control
   Backup & recovery
Companion tools
   For user interfaces
     Forms-based access
     Windows-based access
     Query language
     View mappings
       Re-orderings
       Partial shieldings
       Combinations
   For reports
Multiversion management
   Implicit date/time/user stamp
   Approval, release
   mechanisms

Figure 6.1: Assessment criteria for data management tools

6.3.3 Designing the Data Management Component

Design of the Data Management Component needs to include both the design of the data layout and the design of corresponding Services.

Design the data layout. Design the data layout for flat file, relational, or object-oriented data management.

With flat file data management:

> Define first normal form tables.
>> List each Class and its Attributes.
>> Bring that list into first normal form, resulting in first normal form table definitions.
>
> Define a file for each first normal form table.
>
> Measure performance and storage needs.
>
> Then back off from first normal form to meet performance and storage requirements.
>> If needed, collapse the Attributes for a Gen-Spec Structure into a single file. This will reduce the number of files (in exchange for some added storage space for empty fields).
>>
>> If needed, combine some Attributes into some sort of encoded value, rather than use separate fields. This will reduce the amount of storage needed (in exchange for added processing needed to encode and decode such a field).

With flat file data management with an added twist—using a tagged specification language:

> Define a tagged specification language.
>
> The language consists of tags, a starting mark, a registered item, and an ending mark.
>
> Every PDC Class gets a "tag name" Attribute and a "how I store myself in the tagged language" Service.
>
> Design a parser to reconstitute the tagged language into Objects. The parser includes a registry of registered items.
>
> Key benefit: the structure of the data is in the file itself. It's extendable. It's repairable. And connecting systems can use as much or as little of the data that is needed. And it means

that the data is self-describing; other systems that use the data do not need an extra program for adding the meaning back into the data (something that would otherwise be needed in the flat file or relational approaches).

With relational database management:

Define third normal form tables.
> List each Class and its Attributes.
> Bring that list into third normal form, resulting in third normal form table definitions.
> (Fourth or fifth normal form is fine, albeit a bit esoteric.)

Define a database table for each third normal form table.

Measure performance and storage needs. Then back off from third normal form to meet performance and storage requirements.

With object-oriented database management:

Extended relational approach
> Apply the same approach as described for relational database management.

Extended OOPL approach
> There may be no needed steps to normalize the Attributes. The database management system itself maps Object values into its storage of those values.

Design the corresponding Services. Add an Attribute and Service to *each* Class-&-Object with Objects to be stored. Since such an Attribute and Service applies to each of these Objects, treat each as an "implicit" Attribute and Service; that is, leave it off the Attribute and Service layers of the OOD model, and describe it in the text describing a corresponding Class-&-Object.

With this design, an Object will know how to store itself. The "store myself" Attribute and Service form a needed bridge between the PDC and the DMC. With multiple inheritance, such a tag name Attribute and corresponding Service could be defined and then inherited by each Class that has Objects that need to be stored.

With flat file data management:

An Object needs to know which file(s) to open, how to position the file to the right record, how to retrieve old values (if any), and how to update with new values.

Define an ObjectServer Class-&-Object, with Services to (1) tell each Object to save itself and (2) retrieve stored Objects (search, get values, create and initialize Objects) for use by the other design components.

Note: expect to "batch up" file accessing needs for reasonable performance.

With relational database management:

An Object needs to know which tables to access, how to access the needed rows, how to retrieve the old values (if any), and how to update with new values.

Plus, define an ObjectServer Class-&-Object, with Services to (a) tell each Object to save itself and (b) retrieve stored Objects (search, get values, create and initialize Objects) for use by the other design components.

With object-oriented database management:

Extended relational approach
Same approach as described for relational database management.

Extended OOPL approach
No added Services are required. The database management system itself provides the "store yourself" behavior for each Object to be held over time. Just mark an Object as needing to be held over time, and let an object-oriented database management system worry about saving it and restoring it.

6.3.4 Example—Sensor Monitoring System

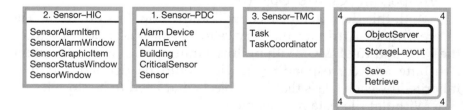

Figure 6.2: Sensor Monitoring System, DMC expanded

The data management for this system is flat file.

A separate file will be used to store the Attribute values for each Class-&-Object.

Files:

Alarm device file

Alarm event file

Building file

Sensor file

with a field SensorType (with values "Sensor" or "CriticalSensor"). Note that the field "Tolerance" has a required value for a critical sensor but a value of "not applicable" for just a (noncritical) sensor.

Figure 6.3: Sensor monitoring system, storage layout description

6.3.5 Example—OOA*Tool*™

The DMC in OOA*Tool*™ uses Classes to store and retrieve Objects held over time with a flat file approach, using a tagged specification language.

Classes

The Classes in the DMC are the following:

OOARoot
    OOATaggedLanguageParser
    OOATaggedLanguageParseTree

    OOAUnloadedDrawing

Figure 6.4: OOA*Tool*™, DMC Class hierarchy

Tagged language and parser

An OOA*Tool*™ model and the drawings (views) on that model are stored using a tagged specification language. The language consists of a tag, a starting mark, a registered item, and an ending mark. The corresponding parser includes a registry of registered items.

In addition, every PDC class has a tag name Attribute and a "how I store myself" Service. The Attribute and Service form a bridge between the PDC and the DMC.

Unloaded drawings

An unloaded drawing holds the name of the drawings that are not yet loaded into memory. This design consideration is done primarily for perceived performance; there is no need to have the human wait while the system loads all related drawings into memory when a model is first opened. Instead, each drawing is loaded upon request. A secondary design reason for this approach is to conserve the amount of high-speed memory that is needed to support a model and its drawings.

7

Applying OOD with OOPLs (or Less Than an OOPL)

This chapter details how to apply OOD with object-oriented programming languages (OOPLs)—or those less than an OOPL.

The issues are addressed in this sequence:

- Being utterly pragmatic about languages
- The language impact on OO development
- Evaluating language syntax and features
- Selecting OOPL(s)

7.1 BEING UTTERLY PRAGMATIC ABOUT LANGUAGES

Object-oriented programming languages (OOPLs) are excellent for supporting OOA and OOD constructs. OOPLs with developer-empowering environments and Class libraries (currently best exemplified by Smalltalk) are the best combinations within this catagory.

"Less than an OOPL" is a practical reality for many software organizations. Such languages, when combined with style guides, discipline, and some perseverance, may still be used to effectively implement OOA and OOD results. No, they're not technically elegant, high-tech sexy, or long-term wins. However, significantly, at least OOA and OOD provide a stable framework for analysis and design results—leading to analysis and design reuse.

7.2 THE LANGUAGE IMPACT ON OO DEVELOPMENT

Every programming language provides some capability for capturing problem domain semantics explicitly.

From an object-oriented perspective, language syntax that captures more and more of the problem domain semantics is very significant, for several key reasons:

• Uniform underlying representation
• Reusability
• Maintainability

Uniform underlying representation. One prime message of object-oriented development is the adherence to a uniform underlying representation that is stable over time. This representation carries through from a problem domain to OOA to OOD to OOP. For example, in a sensor monitoring system:

> Sensor, Building...Classes in a problem domain
> Sensor, Building...Classes in OOA
> Sensor, Building...Classes in OOD
> Sensor, Building...Classes in OOP

Reusability. For reuse to provide significant commercial benefit, one must think of and apply it in a wider sense than just at the programming level. Explicitly expressing problem domain semantics throughout OOA, OOD, and OOP has major strategic advantages. Over time an organization can choose to reuse its OOA results within a problem domain and reuse the corresponding OOD and OOP results, too.

Maintainability. It is next to impossible to deliver two different documents and keep them in agreement with each other—especially in light of the quadruple constraint of schedule, budget, capability, and people. The ultimate documentation is the program itself.

Consider the impact of capturing problem domain semantics within the program itself. For example, in a sensor monitoring system application, an automated tool could scan the program, note the explicitly stated problem domain semantics, and present those semantics to the maintenance team. And the team would see:

> Sensor, Building...from the OOP itself.

So, in selecting and using a language, the issue is not "Which language is most pure?" or "Which language is the truly object-oriented one?" but rather "Which language available to me will do the best job of capturing problem domain semantics?"

7.3 EVALUATING LANGUAGE SYNTAX AND FEATURES

7.3.1 Evaluation Criteria

Language syntax and features may be evaluated by considering support for the following:[1]

- Class, Object
- Generalization-Specialization
- Whole-Part
- Attribute, Service

For Generalization-Specialization, issues include inheritance and name conflict resolution. "Name conflict resolution" is needed to handle the potential for duplicate names within more than one generalization Class and is an issue only with multiple inheritance languages.

For Attributes, issues include support for Instance Connections (part of the state of an Object), visibility, and constraints.

For Services, issues include support for Message Connections (portraying Object interaction), visibility, and dynamic binding. Dynamic binding (which could also be referred to as dynamic dispatching) describes the ability of an application to choose or bind a particular Service at run time, right when the application needs to execute a particular Service. This allows for the flexibility of sending a message to an Object (e.g., print) without having to know in advance what Class that Object happens to be an instance of.

As a related matter, an issue for Objects is persistence. Ideally, there would be seamless integration of programming language and data management syntax. Ontologic's extensions to C++ syntax and Servio's extensions to Smalltalk syntax are two strong examples of such a language extension.

The following sections evaluate major languages—OOPLs and less than OOPLs—in light of their support for OOA and OOD semantics:

---

[1]A note concerning "Subjects": In OOA and OOD, Subjects are a means to an end—they are a mechanism for guiding a reader through a large model. In fact, different Subject breakdowns can be used to guide different reviewers. So Subjects are not actually implemented within the code itself.

OOPLs

- C++ and Object Pascal
- Smalltalk and Objective-C
- Eiffel

Less than OOPLs

- Ada
- C (and other procedural languages)

7.3.2 Syntax and Features—C++ and Object Pascal

This section describes two languages that were developed as a syntax extension to an existing procedural language, resulting in C++ and Object Pascal.

Hybrid languages like C++ and Object Pascal introduce the concept of static and virtual procedures/functions. Static procedures/ functions allow the compiler to resolve the procedure/function address at compile time. Virtual procedures/functions, on the other hand, tell the compiler to place the procedure/function's address in a table (yielding dynamic binding), so the procedure/function can be redefined or extended at a later time.[2] This is not an issue for "pure" OOPLs, in which all procedures/functions are considered virtual.

C++

C++ [Ellis, 1990] is a programming language extension that adds object-oriented features to the programming language C.

C++ includes the following syntax and features that support OOA and OOD:

C++—Class, Object

Class, Object ☞ class, object

- C++ Classes possess visibility constructs: a member of a class (variable or function) can be declared either to be **private** (class-

---

[2]Virtual functions raise a performance versus extendability issue. The overhead incurred by virtual functions may be unacceptable in certain circumstances (e.g., real-time command and control); however, a decision not to use virtual functions will sacrifice polymorphism. If a system is constrained by timing requirements, the decision to use virtual functions should be made on a function-by-function basis.

only access), **protected** (class and derived-class access), **public** (all access), or **friends** (class-granted access—friends have access to private, protected, and public parts).

- Variables and functions are called members.
- C++ Classes possess special member functions for object creation (constructor) and deletion (destructor). The constructor function is named the same as the class name and can be overloaded. The destructor function is also named after the class but is prefaced with a tilde.
- Objects can either be statically declared (memory space reserved) or dynamically declared (memory space allocated from system heap).

The following example shows a Class definition and Object creation using C++:

```
typedef    int      CompletionStatus;
typedef    float    SensorReading;
typedef    int      SensorAddress;

class Sensor
{
    public:
            enum OperatingState {Off, StandBy, Monitor};
            // Create a Sensor
            Sensor ();
            // Copy Creation
            Sensor (const Sensor& aSensor, int theAddress);
            // Destructor
            ~Sensor ();

            // Access - Dump the Data In
            CompletionStatus    ConvertTo (float theScale,
                                           float theBias,
                                           char* unitsOfMeasure);
            ...
            // Access - Pull the Data Out
            virtual char*       ObjectType () {return (theObjectType) };
            SensorAddress       AddressOf ();
            OperatingState      StateOf ();
            ...
            // Initialize and Monitor the Sensor
            virtual CompletionStatus    Initialize (int theInitSequence);
            virtual void                MonitorForAlarmCondition ();
```

```
protected:
        // Attributes for Sensor - accessible only to derived Classes
        char*            ModelNumber;
        char*            Manufacturer;
        int              InitSequence;
        UnitConversion   Conversion;
        float            Interval;
        SensorAddress    Address;
        OperatingState   State;
        float            Threshold;
        float            Value;

private:
        // Class variable identifying Object type
        static char* theObjectType  = "Sensor";

        SensorReading      Sample ();
        CompletionStatus   SetModelNumber (char* aModelNumber);
        CompletionStatus   SetManufacturer (char* aManufacturer);
        ...
};

// static declaration using 1st constructor
Sensor IntruderSensor;

// dynamic declaration using 2nd constructor
Sensor* DoorSensor = new Sensor (WindowSensor, 0x153000);
// (where 0x153000 would be the hexadecimal address of a sensor)
```

C++—*Generalization-Specialization*

Generalization-Specialization ☞ base-derived

- C++ supports both single and multiple inheritance.
- A derived class can declare its inheritance to be **public** (all inherited base class members are public in the derived class) or **private** (all inherited base class members are private in the derived class).
- Class member may be declared as **static**, meaning there is only one copy of the static member, shared by all objects in a program.

Defining a specialization Class using C++:

```
class CriticalSensor : public Sensor
{
    public:

            // Create and Destroy a CriticalSensor
            CriticalSensor ();
            CriticalSensor (const CriticalSensor& aSensor, int theAddress);
            ~CriticalSensor ();

            // Access - Pull the Data Out
            float  ToleranceOf ();

            // Redefine Monitor member function to incorporate a Tolerance
            void  MonitorForAlarmCondition ();

    protected:
            float  Tolerance;

    private:
            // Access - Dump the Data In
            CompletionStatus    SetTolerance (float theTolerance);
};
```

C++—Whole-Part

Whole-Part ☞ nested objects or embedded pointers

- C++ can support the principle of Whole-Part using either nested objects or embedded pointers implementing the mapping between Objects.
- C++ supports defining Classes within Classes.

The Whole-Part Structure constraints between a building and sensor(s) may be implemented by adding Attributes and Services to each Class. For example:

```
class Sensor
{
    public:
            Building     BuildingAttachedTo ();
    protected:
            Building     AssociatedBuilding;
};
```

Within the Building Class, a collection Attribute, BuildingSensors, is introduced to implement the connections between a building and its corresponding sensors.

```
class Building
{
    public:
        char*       EmergencyNumberOf ();
        char*       StreetAddressFor ();
        Sensor      CurrentlyActiveSensor (Set aCollectionOfSensors);

    protected:
        Set         BuildingSensors;
    ...
};
```

For an Object warehouseBuilding, an instance of the Class Building, the following composite statement can be used to obtain the state of a sensor attached to the building:

```
theStateOf = warehouseBuilding.CurrentlyActiveSensor
             (BuildingSensors).StateOf();
```

C++—Attribute, Service

Attribute ☞ variable (data member)

- Visibility: **private**(class-only access), **protected** (class and derived-class access), **public** (all access), or **friend** (class-granted access—friends have access to private, protected, and public parts).
- A class variable can be declared as **static**. There is only one instance of the static variable for *all* the objects within the class.
- Instance Connections are implemented in C++ using pointers. For a range, a collection (array, linked list, etc.) is needed to implement the connections.

Service ☞ member function

- Constructors and destructors must have the same name as the class. They can be overloaded—it is possible to have two or more constructors for a class. Destructors are preceded by a tilde.
- Message Connection can be thought of as a function call, with strongly typed arguments.
- C++ does not support generics (parameterized types). Types must be resolved at compile time.

- Visibility: all (**public**) derived Classes (**protected**), within the same Class (**private**), only to granted Classes (declared via "**friend**" functions).
- No explicit constraints.
- Dynamic binding applies only to those functions explicitly declared as "**virtual**."
- A function can be extended by a derived class only if it has been defined as virtual in the base class.

The following example shows a C++ implementation of the MonitorForAlarmCondition Service for the Sensor Class.

```
void Sensor::MonitorForAlarmCondition ();
{
    float          SensorReading = 0.0;
    AlarmDevice*   WarningAlarmDevice = NULL;
    AlarmEvent*    WarningAlarmEvent = NULL;

    // precondition: State = StandBy
    if (StateOf () != StandBy)
            ReportError ("Invalid State");
    else
    {
        this.WaitForMonitor ();      // trigger on State = Monitor
        while (StateOf () == Monitor)
        {
            delay (Interval);
            SensorReading = Sample ();
            Value = (Conversion.Convert (SensorReading));
            if (Value >= ThresholdOf ())
            {
                WarningAlarmDevice = new AlarmDevice ();
                WarningAlarmEvent = new AlarmEvent ();
                // Record Sensor causing the alarm event and activate
                // alarm
                WarningAlarmEvent->RecordEvent (Value, Threshold);
                WarningAlarmDevice->Activate ();
            }
        }
    };
    delete WarningAlarmDevice;
    delete WarningAlarmEvent;
};
```

Object Pascal

Object Pascal [Ezzell, 1989] is a programming language extension that adds syntax to Pascal.

Object Pascal includes the following syntax and features that support OOA and OOD.

Object Pascal—Class, Object

Class, Object ☞ object type, object

- Class definition in Object Pascal is much like a Pascal "record" definition. The addition of the **object** construct allows for variables and procedures/functions to be treated as an intrinsic whole.

- All variables and procedures/functions are visible to descendant object types and users of an object type. No additional visibility mechanisms are provided.

- Object Pascal adds special constructor and destructor functions for object creation and deletion.

The following example shows a Class definition and Object creation using Object Pascal:

```
const
      Len255 = 255;

type
      OperatingState = (Off, StandBy, Monitor);
      Str255 = packed array [1...Len255] of char;

      Sensor = object
            theObjectType      : Str255;
            ModelNumber        : Str255;
            Manufacturer       : Str255;
            InitSequence       : Integer;
            UnitConversion     : Conversion;
            Address            : Integer;
            Interval           : Real;
            State              : OperatingState;
            Threshold          : Real;
            Value              : Real;

      { Create and Destroy a Sensor }
```

```
    constructor Create;
    destructor  Destroy;

    { Access - Dump the Data In }
    procedure ConvertTo (theScale, theBias : Real;
                            unitsOfMeasure : Str255);
    procedure SetModelNumber (theNumber : Str255);
    procedure SetManufacturer  (theManufacturer : Str255);
        ...

    { Access - Pull the Data Out }
    function ObjectType : Str255;
    function AddressOf  : Integer;
    function StateOf     : OperatingState;
        ...
    { More Complex Services }
    procedure  Initialize (theInitSequence : Integer); virtual;
    function    Sample : Real;
    procedure  MonitorForAlarmCondition (); virtual;
  end;

var
    IntruderSensor    : Sensor; { static allocation }
    WindowSensor     : ^Sensor; { dynamic allocation }
...
begin
    IntruderSensor.Create;
    New (WindowSensor, Create); { allocate space and create }
        ...
  end.
```

Object Pascal—Generalization-Specialization

Generalization-Specialization ☞ ancestor-descendant

- Object Pascal allows inheritance hierarchies (single inheritance) and prohibits lattices (multiple inheritance).
- An object's variables or procedures/functions can be redefined in a specialization or descendant object type, but there is no construct for renaming to resolve conflicts.
- Object Pascal provides for the encapsulation of data and process within an object but does not enforce the encapsulation.

Defining a specialization Class using Object-Pascal:

```
type
        CriticalSensor(Sensor) = object
                Tolerance : Real;

                { Create and Destroy for CriticalSensor }
                constructor Create;
                destructor  Destroy;

                { Access - Dump the Data In }
                procedure SetTolerance (theTolerance : Real);
                    ...
                { Access - Pull the Data Out }
                function ToleranceOf () : Real;
                    ...
                { Redefine Monitor for a Critical Sensor }
                procedure MonitorForAlarmCondition ();

        end;
```

Object Pascal—Whole-Part

Whole-Part ☞ embedded pointers

• The Whole-Part Structure can be implemented in Object Pascal by embedding object pointer variables within other objects.

In Object-Pascal, like C++, the Whole-Part Structure between a building and sensor(s) may be implemented by adding Attributes and Services to each Class that describe the mapping. For example:

```
type
        Sensor = object
                AssociatedBuilding              :Building;

                function BuildingAttachedTo      :Building;

        Building = object
                Set                             :BuildingSensors;
    ...
                function EmergencyNumberOf       :Str255;
                function StreetAddressFor        :Str255;
                function CurrentlyActiveSensor (Set aCollectionOfSensors) : Sensor;
    ...
        end;
```

Again, a composite statement can be used to obtain the state of a sensor attached to the building:

```
theStateOf := wareHouseBuilding.CurrentlyActiveSensor
        (BuildingSensors).StateOf ();
```

Object Pascal—Attribute, Service

Attribute ☞ variable

- Variables are visible to all program units. Encapsulation of variables within an Object is not enforced.
- Instance Connection ☞ collection of typed pointers.
- No explicit constraints.

Service ☞ procedure, function

- Services are visible to all program units.
- Dynamic binding applies only to those procedures or functions explicitly declared as "virtual."
- Virtual procedure or function: a procedure or function should be declared as virtual if there is a possibility that it may be redefined by a descendant.
- No explicit constraints.
- Message Connection ☞ procedure call or function call, with strongly typed arguments.

The following example shows an Object Pascal implementation of the MonitorForAlarmCondition Service for the Sensor Class.

```
Sensor.MonitorForAlarmCondition  ();

var
        SensorReading           : Real;
        WarningAlarmDevice      : ^AlarmDevice;
        WarningAlarmEvent       : ^AlarmEvent;

begin
        // precondition: State = StandBy
        if (State <> StandBy) then
                ReportError ("InvalidState");
        else begin
                WaitForMonitor ();
                while (State = Monitor) do
                begin
```

```
                    delay (Interval);
                    SensorReading := Sample ();
                    Value := Conversion.Convert (SensorReading);
                    if (Value >= Threshold) then
                    begin
                              New (WarningAlarmDevice, Create);
                              New (WarningAlarmEvent, Create);
                              WarningAlarmDevice^.Activate ();
                              WarningAlarmEvent^.RecordEvent
                                          (Value, Threshold);
                    end
              end
          end;
          WarningAlarmDevice^.Destroy;
          WarningAlarmEvent^.Destroy;
      end;
```

7.3.3 Syntax and Features—Smalltalk and Objective-C

This section describes Smalltalk and a language that borrowed heavily from it—Objective-C.

Smalltalk

Smalltalk [Goldberg, 1989] was one of the very first OOPLs. It was originally developed by members of the Software Concepts Group at Xerox PARC and was first released in the early 1970s.

Smalltalk includes the following syntax and features that support OOA and OOD.

Smalltalk—Class, Object

Class, Object ☞ class, object (instance)

- Smalltalk classes are normally entered using the Smalltalk browser.
- An object can access its own instance variables, but not those of any other object.
- Smalltalk objects are said to have a protocol description that describes the messages understood by the object. The methods make up the protocol.

The following example shows Class definition and Object creation using Smalltalk. The content to be entered using the Smalltalk browser includes:

```
class name          Sensor
superclass          Object
instance variables  modelNumber, manufacturer, initSequence,
                    conversion, interval, address, state, threshold, value
class variables     ObjectType
class methods       new, theObjectType
instance methods
        setModelNumber: aString
        setManufacturer: aString
        convertTo: theUnits scale: theScale bias: theBias

        ...

        addressOf
        stateOf

        ...

        initialize: theInitSequence
        sample
        monitorForAlarmCondition

intruderSensor := Sensor new
```

Smalltalk—Generalization-Specialization

Generalization-Specialization ☞ superclass-subclass

- Single inheritance (hierarchies).
- Smalltalk classes are derived from a class called "Object" if they do not inherit from any other superclass.

Defining a specialization Class using Smalltalk:

```
class name          CriticalSensor
superclass          Sensor
instance variables  tolerance
class variables     ObjectType
class methods
instance methods
     setTolerance: aNumber
     toleranceOf

     ...

     monitorForAlarmCondition
```

Smalltalk—Whole-Part

Whole-Part ☞ nested objects

- Smalltalk's collection classes can be used to implement Whole-Part Structures.

Unlike most languages (other OOPLs, package-oriented, or procedural), Smalltalk provides a robust library of software components. With the aid of the collection Classes within the Smalltalk library, Whole-Part Structures are fairly easy to implement. Attributes and Services are added to each Class to implement the constraints. For example:

> | *class name* | Sensor |
> | *superclass* | Object |
> | *instance variables* | associatedBuilding |
> | *class methods* | |
> | *instance methods* | |
> | | buildingAttachedTo |

Within the Building Class, the Attribute buildingSensors is added. The Attribute buildingSensors is an Object of the Class Set, which is defined in the Smalltalk Class library. The Service currentSensor returns a Sensor from the buildingSensors set.

> | *class name* | Building |
> | *superclass* | Object |
> | *instance variables* | emergencyNumber, streetAddress, buildingSensors |
> | *class methods* | |
> | *instance methods* | |
> | | emergencyNumberOf |
> | | addressOf |
> | | currentlyActiveSensor: aSet |

The following composite message can be sent to obtain the state of a sensor attached to a building:

> theStateOf := warehouseBuilding currentlyActiveSensor:buildingSensors stateOf.

Smalltalk—Attribute, Service

Attribute ☞ instance variable

- Instance Connection ☞ collection of object identifiers, implemented using collection classes.

- Visible to methods defined of that class.
- No explicit constraints.

Service ☞ method

- Message Connection ☞ message, with implicit, literature-based protocols.
- Visible to methods defined in any class.
- No explicit constraints.
- Dynamic binding applies at all times.

The following example shows a Smalltalk implementation of the MonitorForAlarmCondition Service for the Sensor Class.

monitorForAlarmCondition

```
"Monitor Sensor at interval, continually checking threshold"

| sensorReading warningAlarmDevice warningAlarmEvent delay |
delay := 0.
"Precondition: State = Standby"
self stateOf = #StandBy
ifFalse: [self ReportError: ('Invalid State:' state)]
ifTrue: [
        self waitForMonitor.
        [self stateOf = #Monitor] whileTrue:
                [ Time delayFor: (delay - Time millisecondClockValue).
                sensorReading := self sample.
                delay := Time millisecondClockValue + interval.
        self value: (self conversion convert: sensorReading).
        self valueOf >= self thresholdOf
                ifTrue: [
                        warningAlarmDevice := AlarmDevice new.
                        warningAlarmEvent := AlarmEvent new.
                        warningAlarmDevice activate.
                        warningAlarmEvent record: self
                            valueOf limit: self thresholdOf]]].
                "no explicit delete is required"
                "(automatic garbage collection)"
```

Objective-C

Objective-C [Cox, 1986] is a programming language derived from Smalltalk. It was written not for the purpose of solving C's shortcomings but to provide developers with a tool for building software components.

Objective-C includes the following syntax and features that support OOA and OOD.

Class, Object ☞ class (factory object), object

- A class definition is split into two parts (interface and implementation).
- Class methods are prefaced with a plus (+) and instance object (methods) are prefaced with a minus (-).
- Objects can be statically or dynamically allocated.
- Objective-C supports dynamically typed objects (i.e., the type is not known at compile time) through the use of a new type: **id**.

Objective-C—Class, Object

The following example shows a Class definition and Object creation using Objective-C:

```
@interface Sensor : Object
{
        // instance variable declarations
        char    *           objectType;
        char    *           modelNumber;
        char    *           manufacturer;
        int                 initSequence;
        UnitConversion  conversion;
        float               Interval;
        int                 address;
        OperatingState  state;
        float               threshold, value;
}
// method declarations
+new; // a Class method denoted with a plus
- delete; // an instance method denote with a minus

// Access - Dump the Data In
- convertTo: (char *) theUnits scale: (float) theScale bias: (float) theBias ;
- setModelNumber: (char *) theNumber;
- setManufacturer: (char *) theManufacturer;
        ...
```

```
// Access - Pull the Data Out
- (int) addressOf;
- (OperatingState) stateOf;
...


// More Complex Services
- initialize: (int) theInitSequence;
- sample;
- monitorForAlarmCondition;
...
@end

Sensor IntruderSensor // static allocation
Sensor *WindowSensor; // dynamic allocation - pointer
IntruderSensor = [Sensor create];
```

Objective-C—Generalization-Specialization

Generalization-Specialization ☞ superclass-subclass

- Single inheritance.
- Nonspecialized classes, like Smalltalk, are derived from a class called "Object".

Defining a specialization Class using Objective-C:

```
@interface CriticalSensor : Sensor
{
      // instance variable declarations
      float tolerance;
}
// method declarations
+create; // a class method denoted with a plus

// Access methods - Dump the Data In
- setTolerance: (float) theTolerance;
...
// Access methods - Pull the data Out
- (float) toleranceOf;

// Redefine Monitor for a CriticalSensor
- monitorForAlarmCondition;
...
@end
```

Objective-C—Whole-Part

Whole-Part ☞ nested objects

- Objective-C's collection classes can be used to implement Whole-Part Structures.

Objective-C, like Smalltalk, provides libraries (foundation and user-interface Class libraries) of software components that can be used to increase productivity during software development. Given the Whole-Part Structure between a sensor and building, the Structure may be implemented in Objective-C using the following:

```
@interface Sensor : Object
{
        // the building to which the sensor is attached
        Building associatedBuilding;
}
// method to return the associated building
- (Building) buildingAttachedTo;
...
};

@interface Building : Object
{
        // Collection of sensors for the building
        Set buildingSensors;
}
// method to return an active building sensor
- (Sensor) currentlyActiveSensor: aSet
@end

theStateOf = [ [warehouseBuilding currentlyActiveSensor:
                buildingSensors ] stateOf ] ;
```

Objective-C—Attribute, Service

Attribute ☞ instance variable

- Objective-C supports two categories of instance variables "@private" and "@public." Absence of the keyword public means all instance variables are private.
- Instance Connection ☞ collection of Object identifiers.
- Visible only to the methods defined in the same Class (if global, visible to the methods defined in any Class).
- No explicit constraints.

Service ☞ method

- Service visibility: Class (factory) methods are visible only to methods defined in the same class, plus methods defined in sub-classes of that class.

   Instance methods are visible only to methods defined in the same class.

- Dynamic binding applies at all times.

- Message Connection ☞ message, with implicit, literature-based protocols. A method returns a value the same way as C function, with a return statement. Messages are within brackets, enclosing a receiver, a selector, and optional arguments (e.g., [IntruderSensor theAddress: 153000]).

- No explicit constraints.

The following example shows an Objective-C implementation of the MonitorForAlarmCondition Service for the Sensor Class.

@implementation Sensor : Object

```
// Monitor the Sensor - checking for an exceeding threshold
- monitorForAlarmCondition {
        // local variables
        float            sensorReading;
        AlarmDevice      WarningAlarmDevice;
        AlarmEvent       WarningAlarmEvent;

        // precondition: State = StandBy
        if ( [ self stateOf ] != StandBy)
             [ self ReportError: "InvalidState" ];
        else {
             // trigger on State = monitor
             [ self waitForMonitor ];
             while ([ self stateOf ] == Monitor)
             {
                     delay (interval);
                     sensorReading = [ self sample ];
                     [ self value: conversion convert: sensorReading ] ];
                     if ([ self valueOf ] >= [ self thresholdOf ])
                     {
                             [ WarningAlarmDevice new ];
                             [ WarningAlarmEvent new ];
```

```
                       [ WarningAlarmDevice activate ];
                       [ WarningAlarmEvent record: [ self valueOf ]
                          limit: [ self thresholdOf ] ];
                       [ WarningAlarmDevice delete ];
                       [ WarningAlarmEvent delete ];
                  }
              }
         };
```

7.3.4 Syntax and Features—Eiffel

Eiffel

Eiffel [Meyer, 1988] is the most carefully engineered object-oriented programming language. It adds a number of capabilities beyond other languages and yet still uses a syntax familiar to conventional programming languages.

Eiffel includes the following syntax and features that support OOA and OOD.

Eiffel—Class, Object

Class, Object ☞ class, object

- Eiffel introduces the notion of features (i.e., variables and routines) associated with a class and object. Users of the class are unaware of the time vs. space trade-offs the class designer had made.

- Eiffel's **export** clause controls access to a class's features—any feature not exported is private to the class and its objects.

- Eiffel has predefined rules for object creation. If a class designer does not explicitly initialize values during object creation, Eiffel will.

The following example shows a Class definition and Object creation using Eiffel:

```
class Sensor export
       convertTo,
       setModelNumber,
       setManufacturer,
       ...
```

```
        addressOf,
        stateOf,
        ...
        initialize,
        monitorForAlarmCondition,
        ...

feature
        type OperatingState = (Off, StandBy, Monitor);

        objectType              : String;
        modelNumber             : String;
        manufacture             : String;
        initSequence            : Integer;
        conversion              : UnitConversion;
        address                 : Integer;
        Interval                : Real;
        state                   : OperatingState;
        threshold               : Real;
        value                   : Real;

        initialize (theInitSequence : Integer) is
        -- initialize a new Sensor
                do
                ...
                end;

        sample is
        -- sample the actual Sensor
                do
                ...
                end;

        MonitorForAlarmCondition is
                -- Monitor the Sensor
                do
                ...
                end;
        ...
end -- class Sensor

IntruderSensor : Sensor;
IntruderSensor.Create;
```

Eiffel—Generalization-Specialization

Generalization-Specialization ☞ ancestor-descendant

- Eiffel supports multiple inheritance: the "inherit" clause is used to explicitly declare ancestor classes.
- Eiffel allows a feature to be redefined: unless a feature is deferred it must be listed in the "redefine" clause in a descendant Class.
- Name conflict resolution is accomplished by using the "rename" clause.

Defining a specialization Class using Eiffel:

```
class CriticalSensor export
      tolerance,
      monitorForAlarmCondition
inherit
      Sensor
              redefine monitorForAlarmCondition
feature
      tolerance    : Real;

      monitorForAlarmCondition is
          -- Monitor the CriticalSensor
          do
          ...
          end;
      ...
end; -- class CriticalSensor
```

Eiffel—Whole-Part

Whole-Part ☞ nested objects or embedded pointers

- Eiffel can support the principle of Whole-Part using either nested objects or embedded pointers implementing the mapping between Objects.

Given the Whole-Part Structure between a building and a sensor, the constraints may be implemented in Eiffel by adding Attributes and Services to each Class that describe the mapping. For example:

```
class Sensor export
       associatedBuilding,
       buildingAttachedTo
       ...
feature
       associatedBuilding : Building;

       buildingAttachedTo : Building is
       do
       ...
       end;
end;

class Building export
       buildingSensors
       currentlyActiveSensor,
       attachSensor,
       ...
feature
       buildingSensors : Set;

       currentlyActiveSensor (aCollectionOfSensors : Set) : Sensor is
       do
       ...
       end;
end;
```

Using an Object of the Building Class, the following composite statement can be used to obtain the state of a sensor attached to the building:

```
theStateOf:=warehouseBuilding.currentSensor (buildingSensors).stateOf;
```

Eiffel—Attribute, Service

Attribute ☞ variable

- Instance Connection ☞ embedded objects, collection of typed pointers.
- Visible to functions in any class (export) or only within the same class.
- No explicit constraints.

Service ☞ routine

- Routine visibility is controlled with the export clause.
- Explicit constraints through assertions:

    precondition with "require"

    postcondition with "ensure"

    loop invariant with "invariant".

- Eiffel supports parameterized types.
- Dynamic binding applies at all times.
- Message Connection ☞ routine call.

The following example shows an Eiffel implementation of the MonitorForAlarmCondition Service for the Sensor Class.

```
MonitorForAlarmCondition is
    -- Monitor the Sensor
    local
            theTime            : Time;
            delay              : Real;
            sensorReading      : Real;
            warningAlarmDevice : AlarmDevice;
            warningAlarmEvent  : AlarmEvent;
    require
            State = StandBy;
    do
            theTime.create;
            delay := 0;
            Current.waitForMonitor;
            from
                    State = Monitor
            until
                    State != Monitor
            loop
                    -- Obtain reading at appropriate interval
                    theTime.Delay (delay - theTime.currentTime);
                    sensorReading := Current.sample;
                    delay := theTime.currentTime + interval;
                    Current.value := (Conversion.convert (sensorReading);
                    if (Current.value >= Current.threshold) then
                            warningAlarmDevice.create;
                            warningAlarmEvent.create;
                            warningAlarmDevice.Activate;
                            warningAlarmEvent.record
```

```
                        (Current.value, Current.threshold);
                -- no explicit delete needed
                -- (automatic garbage collection)
            end;
        end;
    end;
```

7.3.5 Syntax and Features—Ada, a Package-Oriented Language

Ada [US, 1983] is a package-oriented language. It adds a construct to package together some number of variables and procedures. And this construct does give a developer an added advantage over procedural languages.

Ada is not object-oriented. Period. Calling Ada "object based" or by some other euphemistic kindness does not make it any more object-oriented.

Ada is a programming language developed in the early 1980s. It is used on government system projects worldwide.

Ada includes the following syntax and features that support OOA and OOD:

Ada—Class, Object

Class, Object ☞ none

- Ada does not syntactically support the notion of Classes or Objects, but it does support data abstraction and encapsulation through the use of packages.

- Ada packages are split into a specification and body. As long as the package specification is maintained, the body can be changed without affecting users of the package.

The following example shows how to use an Ada package to encapsulate Attributes and Services within a Class:

```
with UnitConversions;

package Sensors is

    type Sensor is private;

    type        OperatingState is (Off, Standby, Monitor);
    type        Str255 is array (POSITIVE range 1..255) of CHARACTER;
    subtype     SensorAddress is INTEGER range 153000...153100;
```

```
subtype      Interval is DURATION range 0.0..999.0;

exception InvalidState;

procedure Create;

-- Access (Dump the Data In)
procedure  ConvertTo
                (self              : in out Sensor;
                 units             : in Str255;
                 scale             : in Real;
                 bias              : in Real);
procedure  SetModelNumber
                (self              : in out Sensor;
                 theNumber         : in Str255);
procedure  SetManufacturer
                (self              :in out Sensor;
                 theManufacturer   :in Integer);
...
-- Access (Pull the Data Out)
function    AddressOf (self        : in Sensor) return Integer;
function    StateOf (self          : in Sensor) return OperatingState;
...
-- More interesting methods
procedure   Initialize
                (self              : in out Sensor;
                 theInitSequence   : in Integer);
function    Sample return Real;
procedure   MonitorForAlarmCondition;
...
private
       type Sensor is record
                ObjectType         : Str255 := "Sensor";
                ModelNumber        : Str255;
                Manufacturer       : Str255;
                InitSequence       : Integer;
                Conversion         : UnitConversion.Units;
                Address            : SensorAddress;
                Interval           : IntervalType;
                State              : OperatingState;
                Threshold          : Real;
                Value              : Real;
            end record;
end Sensors;
```

```
IntruderSensor : Sensors.Sensor;
Sensors.Create;
```

Ada—Generalization-Specialization

Generalization-Specialization ☞ none

- Ada does not support inheritance.
- Some reuse may be obtained using Ada "generics"—parameterized packages and routines.

The following example shows one approach for defining a specialization using Ada.

```
with Sensors;
package CriticalSensors is

    type CriticalSensor is private;

    subtype CriticalTolerance is Real range 0.0...0.5;

    procedure Create;
    procedure SetTolerance (aCriticalSensor : in out CriticalSensor;
                            theTolerance    : in CriticalTolerance);
    procedure MonitorForAlarmCondition;
    ...
    private
        type CriticalSensor is
            record
                theSensor     : Sensors.Sensors;
                Tolerance     : CriticalTolerance;
            end record;
        end CriticalSensor;
```

Ada—Whole-Part

Whole-Part ☞ collection or pointers

- Ada can support the principle of whole-part either using a collection or pointers.

The Whole-Part Structure between a building and a sensor may be implemented in Ada using a collection or pointers. For example:

```
with Buildings; use Buildings;
package Sensors
{
      type Sensor is private;
      function BuildingAttachedTo return Building;

      private
            AssociatedBuilding  : Building;
end Sensors;

with Sensors; use Sensors;
with Set; use Set;
package Buildings
begin
      type Buildings is private;
      package SensorSet is new Set (Item => Sensor);
            — A set is used to hold the collection of sensors in a building.
      function    EmergencyNumberOf return String;
      function    StreetAddressFor return String;
      function    CurrentlyActiveSensor
                        (aCollectionOfSensors : in SensorSet)
                              return Sensor;

      private
            buildingSensors : SensorSet;
   ...
end Buildings;
```

The following statements can be used to obtain the state of a sensor attached to the building:

```
aSensor := warehouseBuilding.CurrentlyActiveSensor (buildingSensors);
theStateOf := aSensor.StateOf ();
```

Ada—Attribute, Service

Attribute ☞ variable

- Instance Connection ☞ typed pointers.
- Ada types can be declared as "private" or "limited private," thus limiting visibility to the routine declared within the defining package. Ada types that are not privately declared are visible to the users of the package.
- Ada supports explicit "subtyping" or type constraints.
- Special error variables, exceptions, can be defined.

Service ☞ procedure, function

- Argument types may be parameterized ones (referred to as "generics").
- Procedures and functions declared in the package specification are visible to users of the package. Procedures and functions declared within the package body are private to that package.
- Ada contains its own tasking model, so a routine can be defined as a "task" and will execute asynchronously.
- Ada explicitly supports exception handling in the event of error.
- Message Connection ☞ procedure call, function call.
- No explicit constraints.
- Ada does not support dynamic binding—everything is resolved at compile time.
- Ada includes explicit syntax for raising and handling exceptions.

An Ada example follows:

```
procedure MonitorForAlarmCondition ();
      SensorReading          : Real := 0.0;
      NextTime               : Time;
      WarningAlarmDevice     : AlarmDevices.Alarm;
      WarningAlarmEvent      : AlarmEvent.Event;
begin
      if (State <> StandBy)
            raise InvalidState;
      else begin
            -- trigger on State = monitor
            WaitForMonitor;
            while (State = Monitor) loop
                  NextTime := Calendar.Clock + Interval;
                  delay (NextTime - Calendar.Clock);
                  SensorReading := Sample();
                  Value := (UnitConversion.Convert
                              (SensorReading, Conversion));
                  if (Value >= Threshold) then
                        AlarmDevices.Create (WarningAlarmDevice);
                        AlarmEvent.Create (WarningAlarmEvent);
```

```
                    AlarmDevices.Activate (WarningAlarmDevice);
                    AlarmEvent.Record (WarningAlarmEvent,
                                        Value, Threshold);
                    -- no explicit delete required
                    -- (variables are statically declared)
          end if;
        end loop;
    end if;
end MonitorForAlarmCondition;
```

7.3.6 Syntax and Features—Procedural Languages

Many languages fall into this category, including C, Pascal, FORTRAN, and COBOL.

The basic idea is much the same: one can apply data abstraction by discipline [Meyer, 1988]. The "data and the exclusive processing on that data" idea can be put into the program with naming conventions and style guides.

As an example for procedural languages, this section considers the C programming language.

C

The programming language C [Kernighan, 1976] can be used to implement some object-oriented features. C's loose typing checking allows this to happen. After all, some object-oriented languages (C++, Objective-C, and Eiffel, to name a few) use C itself as a high-level assembly language.

C includes the following syntax and features that support OOA and OOD:

C—Class, Object

Class, Object ☞ none

- C does not directly support the notion of Classes or Objects.
- The "struct" clause can be used to define variable and corresponding functions (albeit using pointers to do so).

- Memory can be dynamically declared using pointers (space allocated from system heap at run time) or statically declared (space allocated at compile time).

```
typedef      int              CompletionStatus;
typedef      float            SensorReading;
typedef      int              SensorAddress;
struct Sensor
{
      /* instance variables for Class sensor */
      char                 *ObjectType = "Sensor";
      SensorAddress        Address;
      int                  InitSequence;
      int                  Interval;
      char                 *Model;
      int                  State;
      float                Threshold;
      SensorReading   Value;

      /* Create and Destroy */
      Sensor (* Create () );
      void (* Destroy ());
      ...
      /* Access - Dump the Data In */
      void (* SetModelNumber (aSensor, theNumber));
      void (* SetManufacturer (theManufacturer));
      ...
      /* Access - Pull the Data Out */
      char  (* SensorType ());
      SensorAddress (* AddressOf (aSensor));
      int (* StateOf (aSensor));
      ...
      /* More Complex Services */
      void (* Initialize (theInitSequence));
      float (* Sample ());
      void (* MonitorForAlarmCondition());
      ...
};

struct Sensor IntruderSensor; /* static allocation */
struct Sensor *DoorSensor /* dynamic allocation */
```

C—*Generalization-Specialization*

Generalization-Specialization ☞ none

- C does not directly support inheritance. At best, the declaration of a generalization can be embedded in the declaration of a specialization.

```
struct CriticalSensor
{
        Sensor      : aSensor;
        float       : Tolerance;

        void (* SetTolerance (theTolerance));
        float (* ToleranceOf ());
        ...
}
```

C—*Whole-Part*

Whole-Part ☞ pointers

The Whole-Part Structure constraints between a building and sensor(s) may be implemented by adding Attributes and Services that describe the mapping. An additional C-language "structure" is needed, such as a Set, to capture the mapping.

```
struct Sensor
{
        ...
        Building      associatedBuilding;
        ...
        Building (* BuildingAttachedTo ());
}
```

```
struct Building
{
        Set   BuildingSensors;
        Sensor (* CurrentSensor ( aCollectionOfSensors ));

}
```

C—*Attribute, Service*

Attribute ☞ variable

- Instance Connection ☞ array of pointers.

- Visible to all.
- No explicit constraints.

Service ☞ function

- Message Connection ☞ function call.
- Visible to all or just the current source code file.
- No explicit constraints.
- No dynamic binding (although function pointers can be added in).

The following example shows a C implementation of the MonitorForAlarmCondition Service for the Sensor Class.

```
void monitorForAlarmCondition (self);
    struct Sensor *self;
{
    float               sensorReading = 0.0;
    structAlarmDevice   *WarningAlarmDevice;
    structAlarmEvent    *WarningAlarmEvent;

    if (self->StateOf() != StandBy)
        self->ReportError("InvalidState");
    else
    {
        self->WaitForMonitor(); /* trigger on State = Monitor */
        while (self->StateOf() == Monitor);
        {
            delay (self->Interval);
            SensorReading = self->Sample();
            self->Value = (self->Conversion->Convert(SensorReading));
            if ((self->Value) >= (self->ThresholdOf()))
            {
                WarningAlarmDevice->Create;
                WarningAlarmEvent->Create;
                WarningAlarmDevice->Activate;
                WarningAlarmEvent->Record(self->Value,
                                            self->ThresholdOf);
            }
        }
    };
    WarningAlarmDevice->Destroy;
    WarningAlarmEvent->Destroy;
};
```

7.4 SELECTING OOPLS

7.4.1 Which OOPLs Will Dominate?

Which OOPL(s) will dominate in the years ahead?

If one believes the press releases, marketing hype, and quantities of books and seminars, certain conclusions can be reached about which OOPLs will be most significant over time.

And yet the real measure, and almost ultimately the deciding factor, is cost. What is the cost to build a system in a particular OOPL? What is the cost of building reusable program components with that OOPL? How much competitive advantage can an organization gain by adopting one OOPL rather than another? The economic issues, not the religious ones, will eventually declare one or more real winners.

7.4.2 Reusability across OOA to OOD to OOPLs

A key motivation and benefit of object-oriented development is the productivity gains that can be realized through reuse. The fastest and most economical way to develop systems would be to have analysis, design, and programming components that are already developed and tested. OOA to OOD to OOPLs provides a technical basis for building such components.

On reuse, note that object-oriented domain analysis (OODA) is a discipline of applying OOA across a family of potential systems, for example, for all of air traffic control. An OODA model provides a framework for organizing reusable OOA, OOD, and OOPL components.

7.4.3 Class Library and Development Environment

In light of reuse, it seems reasonable that certain "OOPL/ environment/Class library" triads will prove more powerful economically than others, over time. Not just the OOPL but also the environment and the Class library are significant.

One aspect is the development environment. Editors, browsers, interpreters, compilers, and debuggers can be synthesized into a rich development environment.

Another aspect is the Class library. Not just that a Class library exists or does not exist, but rather, what number of useful Classes are available in that Class library? With a significant, mature Class library, less and less new application code need be written. Actually, with OOA to OOD to OOPL, there's a potential of having less analysis, less design, and less programming needed in building an additional system within a known problem domain.

7.4.4 Other Issues

Other issues in selecting OOPL(s) include availability of training in OOA, OOD, and OOPL(s); team-based development tools; human interaction tools; development platform support; delivery platform support; machine performance; memory needs; and ease in incorporating existing software (in any language).

8

Applying OOD Criteria

8.1 INTRODUCTION: WHAT AND WHY

Some methods claim that for a well-specified problem, there is only one "correct" design. That design is not only correct but optimal. Any other design is, at best, suboptimal; at worst, it may not be a correct implementation at all.

To agree with this is tempting, because the claim is usually connected to a companion concept: a *guarantee* that any competent software engineer will produce that one correct design by properly following the method. If it were true, development managers would be relieved of their biggest nightmare: their key designer quitting, joining the army, or being run over by a beer truck in the middle of the design effort, leaving behind no documentation. Whenever this has happened, the new designer—the one assigned to "pick up the pieces"—usually criticizes the previous design as inelegant and inadequate and proceeds to develop an entirely different design.

Perhaps it would be nice to provide development managers with "designer catastrophe" insurance; unfortunately, there is no such thing. For trivial problems, it might be possible that there is only one legitimate design and that all others are demonstrably false; but for large, complex systems, the notion that a particular method will automatically produce the correct design requires an enormous amount of faith.

For large systems, the designer is inevitably faced with making choices between alternatives. Is it better to build the system from components A and B, or would C and D be better? How should the components be organized: in a hierarchy or a lattice? What interfaces should exist between the components? The "architecture" of the system may be based on an object-oriented approach, but that leaves myriad detailed decisions to be made—for which a method does not provide detailed, concrete answers. Depending on how those decisions are made, very different designs can arise, with very different operational characteristics. Thus, the designer must be armed with *evaluation criteria* to help choose between alternatives.

In an interactive development environment, it is tempting not to worry about a formal design evaluation. After all, the designer is so involved with *creating* a design and watching it come to life, that he or she balks at stopping for some dull intellectual work to compare alternatives. If a design proves unacceptable, it can be changed at a moment's notice on the workstation, right? Presto! A new design, a new system.

Though the interactive, evolutionary style of program development is extremely popular in the object-oriented world, it works best when the following conditions exist:

The development environment is fast, friendly, and interactive.

The software engineer is extremely talented.

The software design problem is relatively small, preferably a single-person problem.

The first condition is becoming more common, but it is not universal. *If* you have a powerful workstation that provides half-second response to almost any conceivable command and that has a large display monitor and that has an interpretive or rapid-compilation language, consider yourself lucky. A large part of the software development community works with more primitive tools.

If you consider yourself extraordinarily talented—someone who can hold all of the pieces of a problem in his or her head at the same time—perhaps you can afford the luxury of "design-on-the-fly." Unfortunately, most of us are mere mortals and can well use the benefit of formal design activity before creating a new system. Perhaps certain fiction writers can compose a novel extemporaneously; for most of us, it is well worth the effort to "design" the outline of a book before plunging into the details.

Finally, the value of a formal design—and of design evaluation criteria—becomes evident as the application size grows. For a one-person problem, it's still valuable to distinguish between good and bad designs, but the designer may argue that the choices can be made unconsciously. For two-person or three-person problems, things become more difficult—but if the group works in a close, symbiotic fashion, it may still function effectively while working in an extemporaneous fashion. (This may be little solace to the maintenance programmers who have to live with the product for the next ten years!)

But for large projects, things are different. Nobody supports bureaucracies; and nobody can wait years for a software system to be developed. On the other hand, remember that armies do have a discipline; and even though they are slow, they eventually arrive at their destination. The solo programmer looks impressive until the scale of the problem overwhelms that programmer; when he or she has to bring in a second, third, and fourth programmer to help, communication problems begin to show; more important, emotional arguments about "elegant designs" begin to break out. By the time the system requirements grow large enough to require a thirtieth programmer, the solo programmer's extemporaneous style is a shambles.

So how does one judge a design? What evaluation criteria does one use? To many, a "good" design is one that has the most levels of recursion, or uses the most esoteric features of the hardware, operating system, or programming language. For us, the definition is much simpler:

A good design is one that balances trade-offs to minimize the total cost of the system over its entire lifetime.

Lifetime system cost usually involves such factors as

Analysis costs
Design costs
Programming costs
Test and debugging costs
Hardware costs
Operational costs (people, hardware, etc.)
Maintenance costs

System costs have been shifting away from hardware costs to software and people-related costs for the past forty years. However, the "hardware versus software" battle has to be refought each time a new labor-saving software technology is introduced. And no matter how advanced the hardware technology may be, there will always be a small group whose applications require every last nanosecond of processing time and every last byte of available memory.

Today, with object-oriented systems development technologies, there are complaints about run-time performance, overhead, and slow response time—just as there were when fourth-generation languages and third-generation languages were introduced and when assembly language replaced binary machine language.

If you're building a real-time telecommunications system, performance issues are very real. But now that object-oriented programming languages have matured, a language like Smalltalk continues to close its execution speed gap with C++; and C++ typically has only a 10 percent performance penalty over C. For the vast majority of systems, hardware performance is not a life-or-death issue.

Software costs remain an issue and continue to be more problematic with large, complex systems implemented on cheap, powerful computers. Thus, a good design is usually one that minimizes the cost of creating the design, converting the design into an effective implementation, testing and debugging the system, and maintaining the operational version of the system. Since most software organizations spend 70 to 80 percent of their personnel and software budget maintaining existing systems, one of the most important characteristics of a good design is that it leads to an easily maintained implementation.

The converse of a good design is a bad design: one that does not minimize lifetime costs. But the important philosophical issue here is that one needs criteria for evaluating a design to help *avoid* badness. By analogy, a bridge designer does not ask, "How can I design a perfect bridge?" Instead, he or she thinks, "I know that if I design the bridge this way, it will collapse under certain high-wind conditions; and if I design it *that* way, it may be cheaper to build initially, but it will collapse under certain earthquake conditions." So the act of good design is more a matter of avoiding those characteristics that lead to bad consequences.

8.2 COUPLING

"Coupling" describes the degree of interdependence between people; in OOD, it is the "interconnectedness" between pieces of an OOD. Coupling is important when evaluating a design because it helps us focus on a very desirable characteristic: a change to one part of a system should have a minimal impact on other parts.

In an OOD, look for connections between *Objects* and connections between *Classes*. In the ideal case, examination and *understanding* of one component should have a minimal probability of requiring an understanding of other components. Our colleague Jeff McKenna has a vivid way of expressing this. "If a change to one Class in a system causes changes like popcorn—popping across several Classes—that's an indication that you have too much coupling. You need to ask yourself: What must I do to break the coupling?"

The degree, or strength, of coupling between two components is measured by the amount and complexity of information transmitted between the components. In an OOD design, there are two analogous situations: the coupling between two Objects expressed by a Message Connection and the coupling between generalization Classes and specialization Classes.

8.2.1 Interaction Coupling

Low interaction coupling is desirable. The fundamental guideline is:

Keep the complexity of a Message Connection as low as possible. In general, if a Message Connection involves more than three parameters, examine it to see if it can be simplified.

Three parameters in a Message Connection is not an absolute upper limit; a design exceeding this guideline is not guaranteed to fail. However, the experience of many OOD practitioners suggests that Objects connected via overly complex messages are tightly coupled: a change to one invariably leads to "ripple effect" changes in others.

In addition to minimizing the complexity of an individual Message Connection, one should also simplify the number of messages sent and the number of messages received by an individual Object. For example, the Object labeled ABC in figure 8.1 is tightly coupled with a number of other Objects.

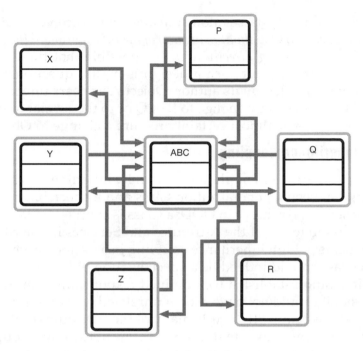

Figure 8.1: A tightly coupled Object

Another example of questionable coupling is known as a "message pass-through." Consider the situation shown in figure 8.2.

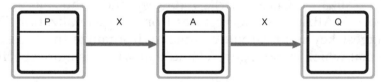

Figure 8.2: An example of a message pass-through

Object A simply passes along the message it receives from P and sends it directly to Q *without using any of the information in the message and without responding directly to it.* It's possible that there is some justification for this, but such a design is highly questionable and ought to be defended by its author. Object A appears unnecessarily coupled to P and Q; any change to P or Q or to the format or content of the message will almost certainly require a change to Object A.

8.2.2 Inheritance Coupling

High inheritance coupling is desirable. Inheritance is a form of coupling between a generalization Class and a specialization Class that one strives to achieve in OOD: a Class is coupled to its generalization Class in terms of the Attributes and Services it inherits.

To achieve high inheritance coupling in a system, each specialization Class should indeed be a specialization of its generalization Class. It should establish a well-defined responsibility; in turn, this means that it should not have a lot of unrelated, unnecessary "fluff." Thus, if a Class explicitly rejects many of the Attributes of its generalization Class, as shown in figure 8.3(a), it is not strongly coupled to its generalization Class. More subtle is the case shown in figure 8.3(b), where the Class inherits many Attributes from its generalization Class but simply doesn't use them. In both cases, the designer should look for alternative Generalization-Specialization Structure in which each Specialization Class inherits and uses—and is thus more highly coupled to—Attributes and Services from its generalization Class. The biggest key is to carefully name and organize the Classes to reflect that which is more general and that which is more specific.

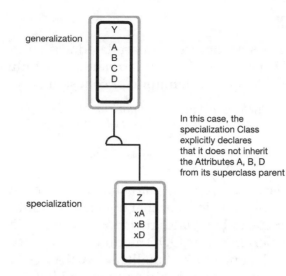

Figure 8.3(a): A specialization Class that rejects certain Attributes inherited from its generalization Class

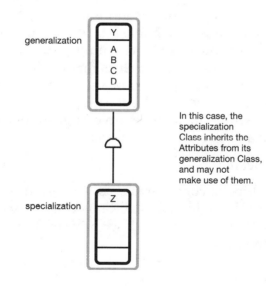

Figure 8.3(b): A specialization Class that may ignore certain Attributes inherited from its generalization Class

8.3 COHESION

Cohesion describes the degree of interrelatedness within a group of people; in OOD, it is the degree of interrelatedness within a group of pieces of an OOD. Another definition of cohesion is:

the degree to which the elements of a portion of a design contribute to the carrying out of a single, well-defined purpose.

8.3.1 Service Cohesion

A Service should carry out one, and only one, function. A Service that carries out multiple functions, or that manages to fulfill only part of a function, is undesirable. One clue is the Service's size: almost all single-function Services in an OOD module are tiny—typically 3 to 5 statements in a language like Smalltalk.[1] A Service requiring 150 program statements, or one with deeply nested blocks, or one with extended "case" statements, should be looked on with a great deal of suspicion!

Another way to gauge cohesiveness is to ask the designer to *name* the Service with a phrase, or English sentence, that describes its responsibilities. Compound sentences, multiple verbs, phrases like "first," or "next," or "after," are all clues that the Service is carrying out multiple functions or a fragment of a single function. It is generally possible to accurately describe the responsibilities of a highly cohesive Service with a single imperative English sentence containing a single verb and a single direct object.

8.3.2 Class Cohesion

The second type of cohesion is Class Cohesion. The Attributes and Services should be highly cohesive—no extra (unused) Attributes, no extra (unused) Services, and all descriptive of the responsibilities of an Object of the Class.

---

[1] These numbers would be different in other programming languages. Note also that (by definition) one cannot know the number of source statements required to code a Service until the code has been written! However, in a typical object-oriented project, code is written much earlier than one would expect to find in a "conventional" project, partly because an OO-development environment may encourage prototyping. Thus, one is likely to have an earlier warning, in an OOD project, of the potential danger of overly lengthy Services.

8.3.3 Generalization-Specialization Cohesion

The third type of cohesion is generalization-specialization (gen-spec) cohesion. Consider the Generalization-Specialization Structure shown in figure 8.4.

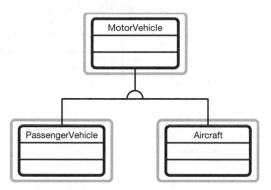

Figure 8.4:   Poor Gen-Spec cohesion

For each of the specialization Classes, these are the questions: How interrelated are the Classes? Does the specialization really portray specialization? Or is it just something arbitrary—out of place within the Structure?

In the example above consider "Aircraft." Does it make sense (applying generalization-specialization) to think about an Aircraft as a kind of MotorVehicle? No. Generalization-specialization cohesion has been violated. Aircraft is misplaced; it should be placed higher in the Structure.

Transport, specializing into MotorVehicle and Aircraft, would be a much better application of generalization-specialization.

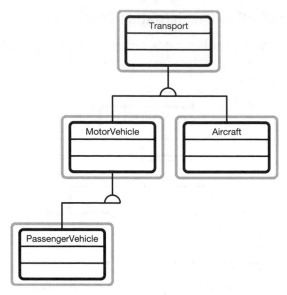

Figure 8.5: Better Gen-Spec cohesion

8.4 REUSE

Though everyone has talked about it since the 1960s, software reusability is rarely practiced effectively. But the organizations that survive the 1990s will be those that have achieved high levels of reusability—perhaps 70 to 80 percent or more.

8.4.1 Why Does It Matter?

The primary benefit of software reusability is higher productivity. In a superficial sense, the software development team that achieves 80 percent reusability is four times as productive as the team that achieves only 20 percent reusability. However, the savings are rarely this great, because the benefits of reusability require

a capital investment to create the reusable components in the first place. This is amortized over the number of new systems that can make use of the components. Obviously, the more often the components can be reused, the less onerous the initial capital investment.

an investment to perform higher levels of quality assurance than would normally be expected for unique software components. Higher levels of QA are required by, and justified by, the higher levels of usage. Most organizations find that they need two to four times as much testing for reusable components than for unique components.

an investment to maintain libraries, browsers, and other facilities so that software engineers can *find* the components when they need them. This can range from a simple index of available components to an interactive expert-system search facility based on key words, etc.

Nevertheless, it is not unusual to see development teams achieving productivity increases of 50 to 200 percent from serious, deliberate application of software reusability.

Another reason to emphasize reusability is *increased quality*. A reusable software component always requires more quality assurance than its nonreusable brethren. But if this is the bad news, the good news is that components with heavy reuse will have higher quality than ordinary components; the bugs are shaken out more quickly and thoroughly.

8.4.2 Why Aren't People Doing It?

If reusability is such a good thing, why aren't people doing more of it? There are four major reasons:

Software engineering textbooks teach new practitioners to build systems from "first principles"; reusability is not promoted or even discussed.

The "Not Invented Here" syndrome, and the intellectual challenge of solving an interesting software problem in one's own unique way, mitigates against reusing someone else's software component.

Unsuccessful experiences with software reusability in the past have convinced many practitioners and development managers that the concept is not practical.

Most organizations provide no reward for reusability; sometimes productivity is measured in terms of new lines of code written plus a discounted credit (e.g., 50 percent less credit) for reused lines of code.

8.4.3 Levels of Reusability

Since reusable code is what everyone talks about, let's start with code.

Reusing Code

The phrase "code reuse" is usually interpreted as making a subroutine call to a module in a library, but it can take any of the forms listed below.

Cut and paste of source code. This is better than no reuse at all, but it is the most primitive form of reuse. The clerical cost of transcribing the code has largely disappeared with today's cut-and-paste text editors; nevertheless, the software engineer runs the risk of introducing errors during the copying (and modification) of the original code. Worse is the configuration management problem: it is almost impossible for the manager to keep track of the multiple mutated uses of the original "chunk" of code.

Source-level includes. Many programming languages have facilities to incorporate source code from a library into a program. Such facilities are referred to generically as "include" or "copy" features. The configuration management problem is somewhat less severe: if the original library code is modified, all of the other programs that "include" it must be recompiled. This presumes that there is some "source code control" mechanism to keep track of which programs use "include"-ed modules.

Inheritance—Object-oriented programming languages include single or multiple inheritance. This adds syntax for capturing problem domain and implementation domain semantics. It also provides a mechanism for reuse via extendability; it gives a technical basis for reuse that is "just like the one before, but a little bit different."

Binary links. With most programming languages, the compilation activity is followed by a "link-edit" activity in which all of the required object modules are collected together. This may include previously compiled library modules that the application programmer invokes in the program. If the reused code is modified, it must be recompiled and reinserted into the library; but for the other programs, all that is necessary is another link-edit to incorporate the modified library modules.

Execution-time invocation. In some environments, the "binding" between a program and its reused library components (as well as the binding between variable names and absolute values within the program itself) does not take place until the program executes. This is particularly common in an interpretive environment.

Reusing Design Results

Rather than reusing *code*, why not reuse a model of the *design* of a program—for example, an OOD model? The most obvious reason for this level of reuse is to facilitate "re-porting" of an application to an entirely different hardware/software target platform.

Or, using the current technology of CASE tools, an existing design model might be (re)used as the starting point in a different design—that is, one that implements the same set of user requirements in a different way. This might be appropriate, for example, if a system was moved from a batch environment to an on-line environment.

Reusing Analysis Results

An even higher level of reuse is the reuse of *specifications*, consisting of an OOA model or some other representation.

This level of reuse would be appropriate if the project team wants to convert a system from an older hardware technology to a newer and more powerful technology. The user requirements might be unchanged, but the internal architecture of the system, as documented with OOD diagrams, could be entirely new.

Other Examples of Reuse

In theory, there is no reason why *all* of the products of a systems development environment could not be reused in subsequent projects. Thus, the project team should look for opportunities to reuse

> Cost-benefit calculations
> User documentation
> Feasibility studies
> Test data sets

Object-oriented component libraries

Code reuse and data reuse are useful concepts, but *object-oriented* reuse will ultimately be more important as OOA, OOD, and OOP gain acceptance in the field.

One of the important advantages of having a library of reusable Classes is that the reuse can be accomplished *not* by modifying existing code (with all of the associated configuration management problems), but rather by *extending* or *specializing* the Classes found in the library, through an inheritance mechanism.

Designware

During the 1990s, some software companies will capitalize on the capability of CASE tools to provide reusable "analysis/designware": a collection of analysis/design models for a specific application that the customer can customize for his or her own unique environment.

Thus, an organization desiring a new insurance system might decide that it is unproductive to solve the insurance problem from scratch, when the problem has already been solved before; on the other hand, the organization might not be willing to live with the constraints of a vendor-supplied package. Until recently, the only option was to acquire the source code from the vendor (often at an exorbitant price) and customize it; this often led to unmanageable maintenance and support problems as the vendor released new versions.

With today's CASE technology, another approach is possible: Why not buy a set of OOA/OOD diagrams and a repository with an initial set of business rules, Attributes, and Services? Customizing could then be done at the specification level or the design level, and the organization could then generate unique code for its needs.

8.4.4 Organizational Approaches to Reusability

The most important ingredient for achieving high levels of software reusability in organizations is *management*. There are three things that management must do:

Provide a reward mechanism to instill a greater awareness of the desirability of reusability. A designer who is being penalized for spending time and effort building reusable components won't do it.

Provide "proactive" leadership to encourage reusability. Many Japanese organizations, for example, estimate the degree of expected reusability at the beginning of the project and then base their budgets and schedules on that estimate; as a result, everyone pays closer attention to reusability.

Change the organization to create a group whose sole job is to create reusable components, rather than take the common approach of hoping that individual software engineers will "generalize" their special-purpose components in their spare time.

8.5 ADDITIONAL CRITERIA

In addition to the major criteria of coupling and cohesion, a number of additional criteria can be used to judge design quality. These include

Clarity of design
Generalization-Specialization depth
Keeping Objects and Classes simple
Keeping protocols simple
Keeping Services simple
Minimizing volatility of design
Minimizing overall system size
Ability to "evaluate by scenario"
Evaluation by "critical success factors"
Recognized elegance in the design

8.5.1 Clarity of design

In every OOD project studied, and in virtually every discussion with OOD practitioners, the phrase "clarity of design" has come up again and again as a criterion of goodness. Our colleague Sam Adams has commented, "A design must make good sense—you should be able to read it as a statement." Apple's Alan Kay put it perhaps even more eloquently: "The Class library whispers the design in your ear."

Clarity is especially important because of the emphasis on reusability in OOD: if another designer can't understand your design, chances are he won't reuse it. As an interesting consequence, Smalltalk programmers are constrained—in terms of the idiosyncratic design style they might otherwise exhibit—by the existence of a rich, common literature and a widely shared Class library. This is somewhat true as well for people working with the MacApp Class library on the Apple Macintosh system; however, it appears to be somewhat less true for C++ programmers, because there is much less of a shared culture, shared literature, and shared library of Classes.

What are the contributing factors in a design that is so clear that *everyone* can understand it? These are the most important:

Using a consistent vocabulary
Adhering to an existing protocol or behavior
Avoiding too many "message templates"
Avoiding "fuzzy" definitions of Classes

Use a consistent vocabulary. The names in the model should correspond as closely as possible to the common names that the reader would expect to see for that component.

Class names in the OOD Problem Domain Component come directly from an OOA model. Class names in the human interaction component will reflect the kind of input-output medium with which the end-user interacts with the system. Class names in the task management component portray tasking. Class names in the data management component will reflect the data management technology.

Consistent names for the Services within each Class are also vital. For example, some Objects have Services whose job is to obtain the value of certain Attributes from a person at the terminal; an appropriate name for such a Service might be "get." If such a name is chosen, all of the Objects should use that name for the corresponding Service—rather than having a cacophony of names such as "input," "read," "obtain," "ask," etc. Wherever possible, make sure that the semantics for all Classes are consistent: if most of the Classes have a "create new instance" Service, then someone trying to learn about (or reuse) the system will assume that *all* Classes have a "create new instance" Service.

Adhere to an existing protocol. The concept of a "role model" is a good one for OOD practitioners to keep in mind. But in fact, the role model probably already exists, because OOD designers rarely work in a vacuum. If there is an existing protocol in the Classes already developed by other designers on the same project, you should follow it consistently.

More commonly, the role model will be evident in the reusable Class library that your project, or your entire organization, uses. The Smalltalk protocol has evolved and has been refined over a period of many years; with other programming languages, the protocol may not be deeply entrenched—but it probably already exists.

Use a small number of message templates. If there is a standard protocol for messages between Objects, then the designer should follow it when designing.

But what if there is no well-established protocol? This could happen, for example, if there is no library of reusable components and if the designer is working alone on a new project. In this case, when the designer essentially has free rein, it is important not to create too many different message formats, or "templates." Where possible, messages should have a consistent format for the benefit of the reader.

Adhere to responsibilities (avoid fuzzy definitions). Our concern here is defining the *responsibilities* of a Class. The responsibilities should be limited and almost self-evident to a reader simply from the name of the Class. As part of a design review, the reviewers should check to see if the responsibilities have been properly defined.

8.5.2 Generalization-Specialization Depth

For a moderate-size system—one with approximately one hundred Classes—you would expect an overall Gen-Spec Structure of approximately seven plus or minus two levels. The programming language will affect the level of factoring (C++ implementations usually lead to more levels of hierarchy), but in any case, it would be unusual to see twenty levels of Class hierarchy for a medium-size system.

Overzealous OOD designers sometimes "overfactor" early in the design effort, creating levels of specialization Classes just for the sake of doing it, rather than trying to make the factoring fit the problem. The consequence is an excessively deep hierarchy that may be difficult to modify later on. Similarly, a common mistake of fledgling OOD designers is trying too hard to specialize off an existing Class. A good "reasonableness" test is to say, out loud, "X (the specialization Class) *is a* Y (the generalization Class)" in an English sentence, and see whether it makes sense.

8.5.3 Keeping Objects and Classes Simple

Simplicity is a virtue in any design approach. In OOD, keep Objects and Classes simple; keep message protocols simple; and keep Services simple. Four guidelines are the following:

Avoid excessive Attributes
Focus on responsibilities
Minimize Object collaboration
Avoid having too many Services per Class

Avoid excessive Attributes. In design, you may only need an average of one or two Attributes for each Service in an Object. Approximately two-thirds of these Attributes can be traced back to a requirement in the Problem Domain Component of the model developed from OOA; the remaining one-third is design-oriented.

While this is a common situation, there is no special minimum number of Attributes in a design. If there are many Attributes, the Class is usually too complex and is trying to do too much. Looking for potential Generalization-Specialization or Whole-Part Structure often helps here.

Focus on responsibilities. Designers should avoid "fuzzy" Class definitions; fuzzy Class definitions are an obstacle to design clarity. Fuzzy definitions are also an obstacle to simplicity and cohesiveness.

How do you know whether a Class definition is "fuzzy"? Ask the designer to describe the Class in one or two simple sentences; if there is much arm waving, if the description includes such phrases as "sort of," "kind of," or "and stuff like that," you're looking at a fuzzy Class.

Minimize Object collaboration. Sometimes an Object carries out relatively little processing of its own but *collaborates* (via messages) with a number of other Objects to accomplish something. While collaboration is often necessary, it is something one wants to minimize: with rare exceptions, it would be unacceptable for an Object to collaborate with every other Object in the system in order to accomplish something.

In most cases, one finds that an Object collaborates with only three to five other Objects; this, in turn, usually implies three to five

Attribute values to keep track of the collaborators. Collaborations with seven plus or minus two Objects is a reasonable guideline, both to maintain simplicity and to maintain design clarity.

Avoid having too many Services per Class. In most OOD designs, each Class typically has no more than six or seven public Services—that is, Services accessible from other Classes. In addition, there may be some private Services needed by the Class to carry out its responsibilities.

8.5.4 Keeping Protocols Simple

The vocabulary in a message protocol should be kept as simple as possible. If a message requires more than three parameters, on average, something is wrong.

If you see computer-science jargon in the protocol, it typically means that the Class is something other than what is in the problem domain or in the implementation domain. This often happens when people first begin using an object-oriented design approach after many years of designing and programming in a conventional third-generation procedural language; thus, when C programmers "move up" to C++, there is a danger of seeing computerese protocols.

8.5.5 Keeping Services Simple

OOD Services are typically quite small—at times, even less than five source statements. As an example, Object International's OOATool™ was developed in Smalltalk with an average of 5.5 lines of code per Service.[2] These numbers may be somewhat larger or smaller depending on the language, but in general, don't look for 200-statement Services in an OOD.

If the Service is too large, it may be an indication that the Service has been organized with flags or internal "case" statements. In general: if the Service looks like a block-structured program, the Classes have been poorly chosen: instead of a CASE in the various Services, it's usually preferable to see an appropriate Gen-Spec Structure.

---

[2] This consisted of 1 line of declaration, 1 line of comment, and an average of 3.5 lines of executable code per Service.

8.5.6 Minimizing Design Volatility

One way of judging design quality is to observe its volatility over a period of time. If a change must be made—either because of a change to the end-user requirements, or because of an error or weakness in some part of the existing design—how extensive is the change? Ideally, one would like to see the following kind of "audit trail" of design changes.

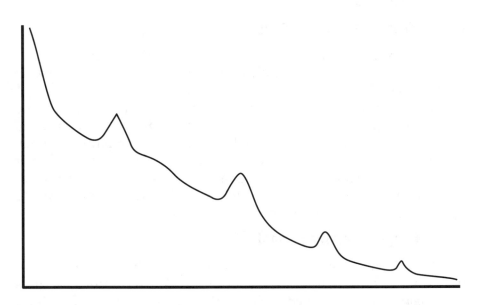

Figure 8.6: Design volatility

Design volatility might be quite high in the early stages of design, as the project team experiments with different designs, throws out early ideas, and gradually refines its approaches. The "spikes" that occur unexpectedly along the way should be localized; if an unanticipated change or design error ripples throughout the system, causing a large spike, it is an indication of poor overall design quality—or bad reuse.

8.5.7 Minimizing Overall System Size

OOD projects are often carried out by lone individuals or by small groups. Small groups can often develop elegant designs even without the formal techniques described in this book, *as long as the overall system is kept within certain size limits.*

For a group of one to six people, a system involving approximately thirty-five Classes or less is eminently "doable"; even fifty to one hundred Classes can be handled by a team of five people and a facilitator, if carefully organized. But a larger system—one with several hundred Classes—requires, at the very least, more people *and* formal OOD notation, documentation, and evaluation criteria. And there is always a danger that the size of the problem will scale up to exceed the ability of the project team to handle it in a clean, elegant way.

So, keep it small; and apply a more disciplined approach—for clarity when small, for survival when large.

8.5.8 Ability to "Evaluate by Scenario"

Another way to judge a design is to "walk through" it with several reviewers. This provides the author and the reviewers an opportunity to test the correctness of the design: *Does it work?* But more important, it should provide an opportunity to evaluate the *quality* of the design: *Can the team find any way to improve the design?*

In the object-oriented world, people find it easy to anthropomorphize Objects. Objects contain both state and behavior. People can imagine themselves as an Object and can attempt to mimic the Object's behavior in accordance with the details of the design they are reviewing. Index cards used as "actor scripts" often work well in this context.

Thus, it is common to hear participants in an OOD walk-through say: "OK, I send the xyz message to you, and then what happens next?" or "How do you handle this situation, when I send you an abc message?"

8.5.9 Evaluation by "Critical Success Factors"

While "correctness" may be a binary decision, quality is not. Nor is acceptability of the final system a simple "yes or no" question. For all but the trivial systems, there are a number of "critical success factors" (CSFs) that will determine whether the system is judged successful and therefore acceptable. Typical CSFs include

Reusability   Readability   Performance

The need to get some portion of the design implemented quickly and available to the user

Thus, the design review could evaluate the OOD design from each of the identified CSFs. Note also that multiple views of the design—perhaps supported with an appropriate CASE tool—could be used to express a variety of CSF perceptions.

8.5.10 Recognized Elegance in the Design

One of the most intangible terms used to describe good designs is *elegance*. Yet the term comes up over and over again in discussions with practitioners; it must mean something! Two useful examples of design elegance in an OOD environment are the following:

> *Repetitions in Generalization-Specialization and collaboration patterns.* When the same pattern emerges over and over again, it suggests that the designer has found a pervading pattern that allows the overall design to be represented in a much simpler fashion.

> *Organization of the design to reflect domain expertise.* The design of the system should reflect the domain itself. If each recognizable "chunk" of the user's problem domain corresponds exactly to a recognizable "chunk" in the design, it will be that much easier to understand.

8.6 FINAL COMMENTS

"Real world constraints," says Sam Adams, "always bastardize the most elegant design. However, people tend to focus on these constraints too soon during design activity. They miss out on the potential 'big win' that is possible through problem domain understanding."

Inevitably, your design will be compromised to accommodate language shortcomings or performance demands or a trade-off between reusability and development costs. But just because your last project demanded enormous compromises from the very beginning, don't assume that this project will. Hardware and language improvements continue to facilitate cleaner and more elegant designs without sacrificing performance. And a trend toward *enterprise productivity* will increase the emphasis on reusable components whose usefulness extends far beyond the current project.

A high-quality design is a statement to the world of your professionalism and your commitment to build a system that everyone can be proud of. Endeavor to compromise as little as possible!

9

Selecting CASE for OOD

9.1 EXPANDING CASE

CASE can be viewed in a much larger context than the hotly publi-cized drawing tools of the present. It would be wonderful to see automated assistance for the *entire* systems development life cycle, which involves over one hundred capabilities; most commercially available products have a maximum of twenty to thirty such capabili-ties.[1]

In the object-oriented world, this means that CASE tools might cover strategic planning, through domain analysis, system analysis, design, implementation (code generation), and testing—from an object-oriented perspective. This also means, of course, that the CASE repository should be able to store *objects* rather than the simple data elements stored in most current CASE dictionaries; the CASE envi-ronment should provide active support for the object-oriented con-cepts of inheritance, encapsulation, and so on. (Some older-generation CASE tools have made a feeble attempt to attach "methods" to the data elements in their repository in order to call their product object-oriented, but they typically don't support inheritance, polymorphism, or message passing.)

This chapter summarizes the basic requirements that a designer needs for OOD support. We also list some advanced features that would be extremely useful.

9.2 WHAT'S NEEDED FOR OOD

Many of the requirements for CASE tools are method-independent. Regardless of the method or notational scheme, for example, modern CASE tools should have graphics facilities for panning, zooming, selection of color schemes, and so on.

In addition to such basic capabilities, CASE support for OOD requires notation, layers, components, and mapping support be-

---

[1] A representative list of CASE functions is discussed in "More on the Future of CASE" [Yourdon, 1988b].

tween OOA results and the criteria-justified changes to the Problem Domain Component, all of which are described in the sections that follow.

9.2.1 Notation

Notation includes the five-layer OOA model and its symbols:

> Subject layer
>> Subject
>
> Class-&-Object layer
>> Class-&-Object
>>
>> Class
>
> Structure layer
>> Gen-Spec Structure
>>
>> Whole-Part Structure
>
> Attribute layer
>> Attribute
>>
>> Instance Connection
>
> Service layer
>> Service
>>
>> Message Connection

and Class-&-Object specification tools, which may include Object State Diagrams and Service Charts.

9.2.2 Layers

Layer support needs to include on/off selection of the five layers (Subject, Class-&-Object, Structure, Attribute, and Service).

It should be possible to collapse a Subject (identifying only its number and name), partially expand a Subject (listing its Class-&-Objects), and fully expand a Subject.

9.2.3 Components

Component support needs to include on/off selection of the four components (Problem Domain Component, Human Interaction Component, Task Management Component, Data Management Component).

It should be possible to collapse a component (identifying only its number and name), partially expand a component (listing its Class-&-Objects), and fully expand a component.

9.2.4 Auto-Tracking Features

Because of the emphasis on reuse, commonality, and inheritance, it would also be extremely helpful for an OOA/OOD CASE tool to have auto-tracking features to map support between OOA results and the criteria-justified changes within the PDC. Similar support could be given for changes to previously developed OOA results within a problem domain.

Many organizations refer to the problem of tracking changes as configuration management. Configuration management is an issue on any large system with many components, many versions, and many developers—but it is an especially important issue when using a method that emphasizes inheritance and reusability of components.

9.2.5 Advanced Features

An important advanced feature is support for reusability. This includes searching, browsing, classifying, and extracting previously built OOA and OOD models and components. Facilities to view, manipulate, and reorganize Class hierarchies would be most helpful.

Another advanced feature is simulation of the behavioral dynamics of the system being modeled. Inbound and outbound Message Connections may be highlighted, based upon the selection of a Service or Services. Alternatively, threads of execution can be displayed—one at a time, or all together, using different line patterns for each thread—once they have been defined by the designer.

A tool might also support inheritance views, with assistance in looking at multiple, single, and zero inheritance patterns.

9.2.6 Model Checks

Model checks provide the designer with early warnings of errors, inconsistencies, and unnecessary complexity. These checks may be done manually (with a checklist, by a clerk) or with the aid of a CASE tool for OOD. When automated, the checks should be project-definable as warnings (a rule that can be broken) or as errors (a rule that one is not allowed to violate).

The basic model checks that should be part of any OOA/OOD CASE tool include the following:

Each Class-&-Object
  has a name.
  has a unique name (within the model).
  has more than one Attribute.
  has one or more Instance Connections.
  has one or more Message Connections.
  has unique Attribute names (within the symbol).
  has unique Service names (within the symbol).
Each Template
  has a specification of each Attribute.
  has a specification of each Service.
  has content consistent with the layers.
  has a usage of reach named input/output within the specification text.
Each Gen-Spec Structure
  has more than one Attribute or Service per level.
  has two to four levels (else getting too complex).
  has Attribute names that are unique within its generalizations and its specializations.
  has Attribute and Service names that do not appear across an entire specialization level.
  has unique Attribute and Service names in generalizations for each portion of a lattice.

9.3 WHAT'S AVAILABLE

As of this writing, object-oriented analysis and design CASE tools are available from a number of sources; others are in progress. Some of the CASE vendors to contact are the following:

OO*Workbench*™, consisting of OOA*Tool*™, OOD*Tool*™, and OO*CodeGen*™
  Object International, Inc.
  Austin, Texas USA
ObjectPlus™
  Easyspec, Inc.
  Houston, Texas USA

Adagen™
   Mark V Systems, Ltd.
   Encino, California USA

Object-Oriented Environment
   Fuji Xerox Information Systems
   Tokyo, Japan

9.4 ADDITIONAL CONSIDERATIONS

Many additional considerations come into play when evaluating and introducing CASE into a project, for example, tool connectivity, team/groupware support, standards conformance, heterogeneous hardware/software platform support, and reusability support. For this book, we'll stick to the OOD-specific requirements for CASE; however, the ideal OO-CASE tool will allow seamless integration of OOA, OOD, OOP, and OO testing.

For the organization experimenting with OOD or just getting started with object-oriented techniques, there may be one other important consideration: price. A relatively inexpensive tool allows the organization to provide automated support while learning about a new method—without feeling that one has made a strong commitment to either the tool or the method.

For additional reading, refer to books and publications that focus on such matters, including *CASE Is Software Automation* (McClure, 1989) and *CASE: Using Software Development Tools* (Fisher, 1989).

10

Getting Started with OOD

10.1 ANOTHER SILVER BULLET?

In a delightful essay entitled "No Silver Bullet" (*IEEE Software*, April 1988), Fred Brooks argued persuasively that there are no "magic" solutions to the fundamentally difficult problems associated with software development. There are no panaceas, no miracle cures that will automatically increase our productivity by a factor of ten while simultaneously eliminating all bugs and software defects. Object-oriented techniques and CASE tools can help—but as several industry pundits have observed, "A fool with a tool is still a fool."

Have no illusions about OOD as a potential "silver bullet." This book stresses the benefits and advantages of OOD, but there is no guarantee that OOD can prevent a project disaster. A recalcitrant user may fail to describe some of the Attributes, Services, or Instance Connections in the system model; a pigheaded designer may bastardize an elegant domain model to save a few microseconds of CPU time.

Any project—regardless of the tools and methods it uses—can suffer the problems of politics, mismanagement, and incompetent personnel. The three most important parts for successful software development are people, people, and people. A corollary to this, observed by Gerald Weinberg, is that there are typically three problems in any software project: people, people, and people.

10.2 IS THIS THE TIME TO START USING OOD?

For some, the issue is not whether OOD will produce miracles, but whether it represents a substantially different approach to systems development that should be adopted as a new standard. OOD is substantially different from functional decomposition, structured design, and typical data-structured methods. But even if it is different and "better," is this the best time to start using OOD? Would it be better for a development organization to wait a while?

Think of OOD as one aspect of an object-oriented "paradigm" or "technology." Most technologies—whether hardware oriented or software oriented, computer related or not computer related—follow an evolutionary curve suggested by figure 10.1.

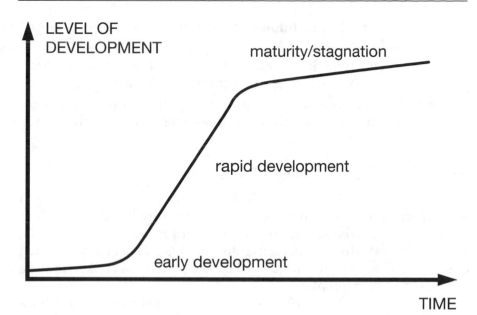

Figure 10.1: Technology evolution

Thus, the "structured revolution" began in the late 1960s with the introduction of structured programming; it advanced rapidly through the 1970s and early 1980s with the development of structured design and structured analysis. In the mid-1980s, some minor refinements were added for real-time systems, and "event partitioning" was substituted in place of top-down decomposition of data flow diagrams. But since 1986, virtually nothing has happened to the method of structured techniques; CASE tools have provided automated support, but the underlying paradigm remains the same.

From this perspective, OOD, OOA, and OOP represent a *new* technology curve; whether the discipline is currently in "early development" or "rapid development" is a matter of debate, but there is little question that object-oriented methods are fundamentally different from the traditional methods used by most organizations.

Thus, the real question that a development organization has to address is: Is this the best time to "jump" off one technology curve and onto another? There are four major issues in this decision:

Is the object-oriented paradigm sufficiently mature and well developed?

Is there a good object-oriented implementation technology available? Does the development organization provide adequate tools for its practitioners to effectively use object-oriented techniques?

Is the development organization sophisticated enough to successfully change its development methods?

Are the systems and applications being developed by the organization the kind that will most effectively use the object-oriented paradigm?

10.2.1 Is the Object-Oriented Paradigm Mature?

Some argue that object-oriented methods are still new and somewhat immature; consequently, they are unwilling to risk their company's involvement in the method until it evolves further. The relative immaturity of object-oriented analysis and object-oriented design, for example, may be judged by the paucity of books, training courses, and CASE tools.

On the other hand, object-oriented *programming* is a well-developed technology; there is a plethora of books, training courses, videotapes, and programming languages to support this approach.

You will have to decide for yourself when object-oriented technology is sufficiently mature to justify pilot-project experimentation or full-fledged support. Obviously, this will also involve your organization's desire to be a "leading-edge" technology-oriented organization, or one that waits until new technologies are well established.

10.2.2 Is There a Good Object-Oriented Implementation Technology?

Object-oriented analysis, design, and implementation can be carried out in a "traditional" software environment, using third-generation programming languages. Realistically, though, many organizations may postpone their commitment to object-oriented techniques until they see a clear path from OOA through OOD and directly into an OOPL.

Consequently, it is common to see organizations adopting object-oriented analysis and design if they are using a language like Ada or Smalltalk or if they view the transition from C to C++ as relatively minor. On the other hand, it is less common to see business-oriented data processing organizations adopting object-oriented analysis and design—simply because it is less obvious how it will work with COBOL.

Yet in late 1989, CODASYL created a subcommittee to recommend changes to the COBOL language to "make COBOL object-oriented." Though the next official version of COBOL is not scheduled to be released until 1999, it is likely that one or more compiler vendors will release interim versions of object-oriented COBOL (which may be known as COBOL++ or OO COBOL!) by 1992. And this development may dramatically speed up the adoption of object-oriented techniques within the business community, regardless of the opinion the OO purists may have of such a language.

10.2.3 Is the Development Organization Sophisticated Enough?

Recently, a great deal of attention has been focused on software "process models." Based largely on the work of the Software Engineering Institute, there is a growing consensus that software development organizations can exist at any one of five levels of "process maturity." The five levels are described as follows:

Initial level (level 1). There is no formal method, no consistency, no standards on how systems should be built. Every software developer considers him- or herself an artist; anarchy prevails.

Repeatable level (level 2). There is a consensus within the organization about "the way we do things around here," but it has not been formalized or written down. The systems development process is statistically stable through rigorous management of costs and schedules; however, success depends on the intuitive skills of project managers.

Managed level (level 3). There is a formal, documented process for developing systems. Software inspections are rigorously practiced, and configuration management is more advanced than at level 2. There is a "software process group" that constantly refines and updates the organization's methods.

Measured level (level 4). The organization has instituted formal process measurements—often referred to as "software metrics" to measure its *process* for building systems, as well as the resulting *products*.

Optimizing level (level 5). The organization uses the measurements from level 4 as a "feedback" mechanism to improve those parts of its process that are found to be weak or deficient.

Usually, an organization cannot make effective use of new tools (e.g., CASE tools) or methods (e.g., OOD) unless it is at level 3 or above. Unfortunately, approximately 87 percent of large U.S. software development organizations surveyed in the late 1980s were at level 1; another 10 to 12 percent were at level 2; and only about 1 percent were at level 3. As of late 1990, no organizations had been found at level 4 or level 5 in the United States.

10.2.4 Is the Organization Building Systems That Will Exploit Object-Oriented Techniques?

People generally adopt a new paradigm to solve familiar problems quickly or efficiently. Because of the cost of making the shift (e.g., training costs), and the natural inertia of humans (as well as the conservative nature of the organizations to which they belong), it is likely that people will continue using older technologies until "order-of-magnitude" improvements are available, *or until new problems appear that cannot be practicably solved with older technologies.*

A case in point: software managers at IBM have commented to one of the authors that all of their attempts to use standard structured techniques to build applications in an OS/2 Presentation Manager environment have been dismal failures; the only successes they could point to were applications developed with object-oriented techniques.

The OS/2 Presentation Manager environment is typical of what many call the "GUI environment" today: a graphical user interface, characterized by pull-down menus, multiple windows, icons rather than textual commands, and mouse-driven commands. In such an environment, the new object-oriented paradigm excels; the older structured approach typically fails.

But remember that not everyone is using a GUI environment. Many organizations still use dumb terminals with character-based input commands; or they may still be building batch systems with card input and magnetic tape output. Walking into some data processing shops is like walking through a time warp and watching the calendar turn back to 1968.

If you spend your days developing the same batch payroll systems you developed in the 1960s and 1970s, and if your only desire is to improve productivity by 10 percent, it will be hard to justify a major transition to object-oriented systems development techniques. But if you are building new systems for which the conventional technologies are demonstrably inadequate, then it may be appropriate to begin using object-oriented techniques.

10.3 REVOLUTION VERSUS EVOLUTION

In many method discussions, OOA and OOD are portrayed as "revolutions" that can completely replace the earlier structured techniques. The lunatic fringe of the object-oriented camp even suggests that all of the software developed with earlier methods is no good and should be thrown out, and that the earlier generation of software engineers who were weaned on structured techniques is unsalvageable and should be put out to pasture.

Another group, the "synthesists," argues that object-oriented techniques and structured techniques are compatible, and that many of the best ideas of both techniques can be used together. As an example, some synthesists point out that the event-partitioning approach of structured analysis can be carried out in such a way as to identify a number of discrete bubbles (functions) that surround local data stores in a data flow diagram. Grouping the bubbles and the data store together is, according to this group, essentially the same as creating objects; thus, *voila!* the system model produced by structured analysis has been "objectified."

There is little doubt one could arrive at the same result using different methods; but it has also been our experience that the thinking process, the discovery process, and the communication between user, analyst, and designer are fundamentally different with OOA/OOD than with structured analysis/design. In that regard, we side squarely with the revolutionaries, though we disagree that older software engineers who began with structured techniques are incapable of shifting to an object-oriented view of the world.

At the same time, we agree with the fundamental message of the synthesists, even though we disagree with many of their examples and tactics. Fundamental concepts such as cohesion, coupling, abstraction, partitioning, conscious deferral of design decisions, and so on are just as relevant in OOD as they were in the days of earlier design methods.

10.4 HOW TO GET STARTED WITH OOD

Getting started with OOD is, in many ways, the same as getting started with any new technology. You must first perceive that there is a problem that OOD can solve that your conventional approach won't solve adequately. Review the motivations and benefits outlined in chapter 1; look for a challenging problem domain that is not easily tackled with older methods, where there is a great need for the system to respond to changes easily, and where there is a need to represent commonality explicitly.

Then you must "sell" the OOD concept to others in the organization: senior managers who must invest money and provide support, middle-level managers who must figure out how to use a new technology while not disrupting their schedules and budgets, and various levels of technicians who may or may not be enthusiastic about adopting new techniques. Pilot projects are a necessity with OOD, as with any other new technology, in order to gain experience and adapt the method to local needs. Training is inevitably required, and a careful implementation plan must be laid out.

Since details of getting started with OOD (e.g., What kind of pilot project? How long will the training take? etc.) are so similar to the introduction of other computer technologies, one can take advantage of existing "technology transfer" strategies. See Yourdon [1988] and Bouldin [1989]. A reasonable OOA/OOD/OOP pilot project could consist of a small team of two or three problem domain experts, two or three analysts, and five or six designers and programmers; with effective OOD tools and OOPL languages, the pilot project should continue over three to six months.

10.5 CONCLUSION

We are enthusiastic about the future of object-oriented techniques, especially OOA and OOD. We acknowledge the importance of many earlier methods, but we have left them behind; nary a data flow diagram or structure chart have we drawn in the past few years. For us, OOD is the future, and the future is here and now.

We hope you feel the same way. You have spent the past chapters reading about OOD. Now is the time to stop reading about it and start *doing* it. And please keep in touch; both authors are practitioners in the field with a commitment to continuing with the successful application of this method on real-world problems. Drop us a note and let us know your experiences. *Ciao!*

Appendix A

OOA/OOD Notation Summary

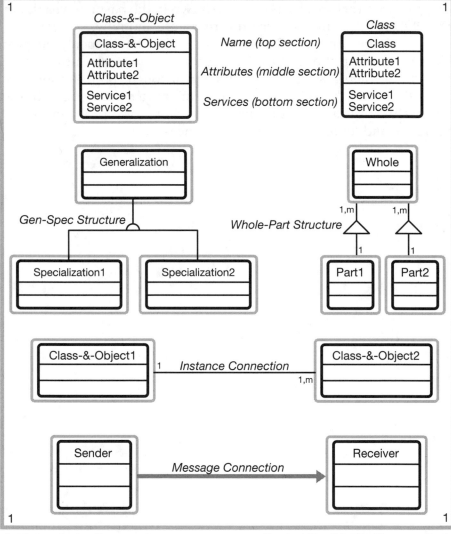

Figure A.1: OOA/OOD notations

Reprinted from P. Coad and E. Yourdon, *Object-Oriented Analysis*, pp. 195-205, © 1991 Object International Inc., by permission of Prentice Hall, Inc., Englewood Cliffs, NJ.

specification
> *attribute*
> *attribute*
> *attribute*
>
> *externalInput*
> *externalOutput*
>
> *objectStateDiagram*
>
> *additionalConstraints*
>
> *notes*
>
> *service*
> *service*
> *service*

and, as needed,
> *traceabilityCodes*
> *applicableStateCodes*
> *timeRequirements*
> *memoryRequirements*

Figure A.2:   Class-&-Object specification template

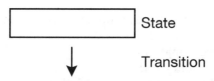

State

Transition

Figure A.3:   Object State Diagram notation (used within the template)

Condition (if; pre-condition; trigger, terminate)

Text block

Loop (while; do; repeat; trigger/terminate)

Connector (connected to the top of the next symbol)

Figure A.4:   Service Chart notation (used within the template)

Appendix B

OOA Strategy Summary

ANALYSIS STRATEGY—Finding Class-&-Objects

Object. An abstraction of something in a problem domain, reflecting the capabilities of a system to keep information about or interact with it; an encapsulation of Attribute values and their exclusive Services.

Class. A description of one or more Objects with a uniform set of Attributes and Services, including a description of how to create new Objects in the Class.

Class-&-Object. A term meaning "a Class and the Objects in that Class."

How to name
> Use a singular noun or adjective and noun; describe a single Object in the Class; adhere to the standard vocabulary for the problem domain.

Where to look
> Observe firsthand; listen actively; check previous OOA results; check other systems; read, read, read; and prototype.

What to look for
> Look for structures, other systems, devices, things or events remembered, roles played, operational procedures, sites, and organizational units.

What to consider and challenge
> Needed remembrance, needed behavior, (usually) multiple Attributes, (usually) more than one Object in a Class, always-applicable Attributes, always-applicable Services, domain-based requirements, and not merely derived results.

ANALYSIS STRATEGY—Identifying Structures

Structure. Structure is an expression of problem-domain complexity, pertinent to the system's responsibilities. The term "Structure" is used as an overall term, describing both Generalization-Specialization (Gen-Spec) and Whole-Part Structures.

Gen-Spec Structures
> Consider each Class as a generalization. For its potential specializations, ask:
>> Is it in the problem domain?
>> Is it within the system's responsibilities?

Will there be inheritance?

Will the specializations meet the "what to consider and challenge" criteria for Class-&-Objects?

Also, in a similar fashion, consider each Class as a specialization. For its potential generalizations, ask these same questions.

Check previous OOA results in the same and similar problem domains.

If many specializations are possible, consider the simplest specialization and the most elaborate specialization, and then follow with the various ones in between.

The most common form of Gen-Spec Structure is a Gen-Spec hierarchy.

Yet a lattice may be used to:

Highlight additional specializations

Explicitly capture commonality

Only modestly increase model complexity

If a lattice structure becomes unwieldy, consider reorganizing part of it into a hierarchy, which may be more effective in communicating the problem domain and the system's responsibilities.

Avoid naming conflicts within a lattice. Otherwise, a specialization that inherits with name conflicts must include the conflicting names, and then resolve what is required in the corresponding specification.

Whole-Part Structures

What to look for:

Consider these variations—

Assembly-Parts

Container-Contents

Collection-Members

Check previous OOA results in the same and similar problem domains.

What to consider and challenge:

Consider each Object as a whole. For its potential parts, ask:

Is it in the problem domain?

Is it within the system's responsibilities?

Does it capture just a status value? If so, then just include a corresponding Attribute within the whole.

Does it provide a useful abstraction in dealing with the problem domain?

Also, in a similar fashion, consider each Object as a part. For each potential whole, ask these same questions.

Multiple Structures

Multiple Structures sometimes touch top-to-bottom; Instance Connections may map them, side-by-side.

ANALYSIS STRATEGY—Identifying Subjects

Subject. A Subject is a mechanism for guiding a reader (analyst, problem domain expert, manager, client) through a large, complex model. Subjects are also helpful for organizing work packages on larger projects, based upon initial OOA investigations.

How to select

Promote the name of the uppermost Class in each Structure upward to a Subject. Then, promote the name of each Class-&-Object not in a Structure upward to a Subject. Check previous OOA results in the same and similar problem domains.

How to refine

Refine Subjects by using problem subdomains. Refine Subjects by using minimal interdependencies (Structures, Instance Connections) and minimal interactions (Message Connections) between them; use the Structure, Attribute, and Service layers to guide you.

How to construct

On the Subject layer, draw each Subject as a simple rectangular box, with a Subject name and number inside. Optionally, list the Classes that are included in the Subject, too.

On other layers, indicate the Subjects with labeled Subject partitioning boxes, to guide the reader from Subject to Subject.

For a large model, as needed to facilitate communication, consider using a separate set of layers for each Subject.

Subjects may be thought of as collapsed, partially expanded (listing its Classes), and fully expanded (Subject partitioning boxes, layered on top of other OOA layers).

A Class-&-Object may be in more than one Subject (when useful in guiding the reader).

Subjects may contain other Subjects, providing multilevel maps to guide a reader through a large model.

When to Add
>   Add Subjects once an overall map is needed to guide the various readers through the model.

ANALYSIS STRATEGY—Defining Attributes

Attribute. An Attribute is some data (state information) for which each Object in a Class has its own value.

Identify the Attributes
>   Questions to ask.
>>   "How am I described in general?"
>>   "How am I described in this problem domain?
>>   "How am I described in the context of this system's responsibilities?"
>>   "What do I need to know?"
>>   "What state information do I need to remember over time?"
>>   "What states can I be in?"
>   Check previous OOA results in the same and similar problem domains.
>   Make each Attribute capture an "atomic concept."
>>   A single value
>>   A tightly related grouping of values
>   Whether or not an always-recalculable Attribute is held over time is a design decision—time vs. memory. Specify the calculation Service, without a corresponding always-recalculable Attribute.
>   Implicit identifiers, "id" (identifier) and "cid" (connection identifier), may be used in specification text when needed.

Position the Attributes
>   Put each Attribute with the Class-&-Object it best describes (check the problem domain).
>   Apply inheritance in Gen-Spec Structures.
>>   Position the more general Attributes higher.
>>   Position specialized Attributes lower.

Identify Instance Connections

Instance Connection. An Instance Connection is a model of problem domain mapping(s) that one Object needs with other Objects, in order to fulfill its responsibilities.
>   Check previous OOA results in the same and similar problem domains.
>   For each Object, add connection lines.
>>   Add subject-matter mappings between Objects,

paying attention to where the connection goes on Gen-Spec Structures.

For each Object, define the amount or range.

The lower bound

Optional connection? Lower bound is 0.

Mandatory connection? Lower bound is 1 or greater.

The upper bound

Single connection? Upper bound is 1.

Multiple connections? Upper bound is greater than 1.

(Note: a multiple connection may imply an Attribute to keep track of the current or most recent mapping, e.g., DateTime or Status)

Use the specification template keyword "additional-Constraints" to capture additional constraints, as needed.

Constrain Whole-Part Structures, too. (The difference is the underlying semantic strength.)

Check special cases

Special Cases with Attributes

Check each Attribute for a value of "not applicable."

Check each Class-&-Object with just one Attribute.

Check each Attribute for repeating values.

Special Cases with Instance Connections

Check each many-to-many Instance Connection.

Check each Instance Connection between Objects of a single Class.

Check multiple Instance Connections between Objects.

Check for additional needed Instance Connections.

Check for one connecting Object (of many) having special meaning.

Specify the Attributes

Name. (Standard vocabulary. Reflects problem domain, system's responsibilities. Readable. No embedded values.)

Description.

Constraints.

On constraints

May reduce the amount of Service specification needed.

Scrutinize cost vs. benefit.

Unit of measure, range, limit, enumeration; default; precision

Create/access constraint?
Constrained by other Attributes?
Traceability code(s), applicable state code(s)
(Option: show such code(s) on the Attribute Layer, for
heightened visibility)

ANALYSIS STRATEGY—Defining Services

Service. A Service is a specific behavior that an Object is responsible for
  exhibiting.

Identify Object States

Examine the potential values for the Attributes.

Determine whether the system's responsibilities include different behavior for those potential values.

Check previous OOA results in the same and similar problem
domains.

Describe the states and transitions in an Object State Diagram.

Identify the required Services

Algorithmically simple Services

Create—creates and initializes a new Object in a Class.

Connect—connects (disconnects) an Object with another.

Access—gets or sets the Attribute values of an Object.

Release—releases (disconnects and deletes) an Object.

Algorithmically complex Services

Check previous OOA results in the same and similar
problem domains.

Two categories

Calculate—calculates a result from the Attribute
values of an Object.

Monitor—monitors an external system or device.
It deals with external system inputs and outputs,
or with device data acquisition and control. It may
need some companion Services, such as Initialize
or Terminate.

Ask

What calculations is the Object responsible for
performing on its values?

What monitoring is the Object responsible for
doing, in order to detect and respond to a change
in an external system or device, i.e., the required
event-response behavior?

Use domain-specific names.

Identify Message Connections

Message Connection. A Message Connection models the processing dependency of an Object, indicating a need for Services in order to fulfill its responsibilities.

For each Object

What other Objects does it need Services from?

Draw an arrow to each of those Objects.

What other Objects need one of its Services?

Draw an arrow from each of those Objects to the one under consideration.

Follow each Message Connection to the next Object, and repeat the questions.

Check previous OOA results in the same and similar problem domains.

Examine Message Connection threads.

Use to check for model completeness (via role-playing simulation, by humans or by computer).

Use to determine real-time processing requirements (when pertinent).

"Real-time" analysis ⇨ performance requirements

Allocate an overall thread budget across the participating Services and Message Connections.

Specify the Services

Check previous OOA results in the same and similar problem domains.

Use a template, with an Object State Diagram and bullet lists/ Service Charts.

Use a consistent text block style.

Express additional constraints.

Summarize state-dependent Services, using a Services/States table.

For heightened visibility, consider putting state codes next to the Services on the Service layer itself.

Put the OOA documentation set together

The Five-Layer OOA Model

The Class-&-Object specifications

Supplemental documentation, as needed

Table of critical threads of execution

Additional system constraints

Services/States table

Appendix C

OOD Strategy Summary

DESIGN STRATEGY—Designing the Problem Domain Component

Apply OOA

Use OOA results—and improve them during OOD

Use OOA results—and add to them during OOD

    Reuse design and programming Classes

        Add the off-the-shelf Class to the PDC

        Identify any Attributes or Services within the off-the-shelf Class that will not be used

        Add a Gen-Spec specialization from the off-the-shelf Class to the problem domain Class

        Identify the portion of the problem domain Class that is no longer needed in that Class, those Attributes and Services now being inherited from the off-the-shelf Class

        Revise the structures and connections to the problem domain Class

    Group problem-domain-specific Classes together

    Establish a protocol by adding a generalization Class

    Accommodate the supported level of inheritance

        Multiple inheritance patterns

            Narrow diamond

            Wide diamond

        A single inheritance language

            Split into multiple hierarchies, with mappings between them

                Mapping ⇨ a Whole-Part Structure or an Instance Connection

                This approach models the Objects of the specialization Classes as a collection of "roles" played out by Objects of a single generalization Class

            Flatten into a single hierarchy

                One or more generalizations–specializations is no longer explicit

                Some Attributes and Services will be repeated in the specialization Classes

A zero inheritance language

Inheritance in a programming language

Is more than syntactic sugar

Provides a syntax for capturing problem domain semantics

Explicitly expresses common Attributes and Services

Provides a basis for reusability via extendability

Each Gen-Spec Structure will need to be flattened into a grouping of Class-&-Objects

Improve performance

Improve speed

Measure, modify, measure again

Fast follows function

Modify PDC for speed reasons only as a last resort

Improve perceived speed

Any of the four OOD Components may add building blocks to cache interim results

Extend a Class-&-Object with Attributes that store interim results

Extend a Class-&-Object with lower-level building blocks

Support the Data Management Component

"Each Object saves itself"

Tell an Object to save itself

Add Attributes, Services to define this

Each Object sends itself to the Data Management Component, which saves it

Tell an Object to save itself

Add Attributes, Services to define this

The needed Attributes and Services

With single inheritance, modify the PDC directly

Add an Attribute to identify the Objects as belonging to a particular Class

Add a Service to define how the Object is to store its values

Keep them both implicit: not included on the diagrams, but defined in text

With multiple inheritance

Put these additions into a new Class, then modify each PDC to include an additional generalization Class

Put an Attribute to identify the Objects as belonging to a particular Class

Add a Service to define how the Object is to store its values

All other Classes inherit from this Class

Keep the inheritance implicit

Each Object to be held over time is managed by OO DBMS

Add lower-level components

Don't modify just to reflect team assignments

Review and challenge the additions to OOA results

DESIGN STRATEGY—Designing the Human Interaction Component

Classify the humans

"Put yourself in someone else's shoes, and stay there for a while"

Classify by skill level

Classify by organizational level

Classify by membership in different groups

Describe the humans and their task scenarios

Who

Purpose

Characteristics

Critical success factors

Needs/wants

Likes/dislikes/biases

Skill level

Task scenarios

Design the command hierarchy

Study existing user-interaction metaphors and guidelines

Establish an initial command hierarchy

Refine the command hierarchy
> Ordering
>> Most frequently used Service appears first
>> In customary work-step order
>
> Whole-part chunking
> Breadth vs. depth
>> Keep from overloading short-term memory limitations
>> Three chunks of about three items each

Design the detailed interaction
> Consistency
> Few steps
> No "dead air"
> Closure
> Undo
> No memory storage in "human RAM"
> Time and effort to learn
> Pleasure and appeal (look and feel)
>> Look: apply graphic design principles
>> Feel: prototype and watch the human

Continue to prototype
> Prototyping the human-computer interaction is essential
> Consider menus, pop-ups, fill-ins, and command shortcuts
> Use a menu-building tool or visual prototyping tool
> Prototype several alternatives.
> Strive for *miroyokutaki hinshitsu*
>> How do you feel at this point?
>> What is it that you really would like next?
>> What command sequence just plain gets in your way?
>> What help do you need to do a more effective job at this point?

Design the HIC Classes
> Window
>> xxxWindow
>> yyyWindow
>
> Field
> Graphic
> Selector

Design, accounting for Graphical User Interfaces (when applicable)

> Typefaces
>
> Coordinate systems
>
> Events
>
>> Direct
>>
>>> An event occurs, and the system executes the corresponding event-handler routine
>>>
>>> A single item in a window may have its own event handler
>>
>> Queued
>>
>>> An event occurs and is queued by the system
>>>
>>> Applications call "next event" to get an event and then take whatever action is needed
>>
>> GUI-independent toolkit
>>
>>> Develop command set as superset
>>>
>>> Use a consistent event model
>>>
>>> Supply and register GUI-specific event handlers within GUI software

DESIGN STRATEGY—Designing the Task Management Component

When needed

> Data acquisition and control responsibility for local device(s)
>
> Human interfaces with multiple windows that may be simultaneously selected for input
>
> Multi-user systems
>
> Multisubsystem software architectures
>
> On a single processor—coordinate and communicate
>
> On multiple processors—needed on each processor, and to support interprocessor communication
>
> Communicate with another system

Identify event-driven tasks

> Certain tasks are event-driven
>
> Such tasks may be responsible for communication with a device, one or more windows on a screen, another task, a subsystem, another processor, or another system
>
> A task may be designed to trigger upon an event, often signaling the arrival of some data from an input data line; or from a data buffer

How it works

The task sleeps, waiting for an interrupt from the data line

Upon receipt of the interrupt, the task wakes up, gobbles up the data, puts it in a buffer in memory or some other destination, notifies whoever need to know about it, and then goes back to sleep

Identify clock-driven tasks

These tasks are triggered to do some processing at a specified time interval

Certain devices may need periodic data acquisition and control; certain human interfaces, subsystems, tasks, processors, or other systems may need periodic communication

How it works

The task sets a wake-up time and goes to sleep

The task sleeps, waiting for an interrupt from the system

The task wakes up, does its work, notifies whoever need to know about it, and then goes back to sleep

Identify priority tasks and critical tasks

A priority task accommodates either high-priority or low-priority processing needs

High-priority Service(s) may need to be isolated into a separate task

Low-priority Services can be relegated to lower-priority processing

High criticality

Some Services may be highly critical to the continued operation of the system under consideration

Some of those Services may be essential for continued operation even during a degraded mode of operation

Additional task(s) may be used to isolate such critical processing

This isolation partitions the intensive design, programming, and testing required for high-reliability processing

Identify a coordinator

With three or more tasks, consider adding another task to act as a coordinator

Such a task adds overhead, and context switch time may discourage this design approach

Such a task brings the benefit of encapsulation of intertask coordination

Use this kind of task to coordinate the tasks, and nothing more

Challenge each task

Keep the number of tasks to a minimum

Key issue: understandability

Define each task

What it is

Name the task

Describe the task briefly

Add a new constraint—task name—to each Service in the OOD components

Assign that constraint a value for each Service in the OOD components

Service splits

If a single Service is split across more than one task, then modify the Service names and descriptions

For Services that include coordination and communication with devices, other tasks, or other systems, expand the Service specification with protocol-specific detail

How it coordinates

Indicate whether the task is event-driven or clock-driven

For event-driven tasks, describe the event(s) that trigger(s) it

For clock-driven tasks, describe the time interval to elapse before the task is triggered, and indicate whether it is a one-time interval or a repeating one

How it communicates

From what does the task get its values?

Where does the task send its values?

A template

Name

Description

Priority

Services included

Coordinates by

Communicates via

DESIGN STRATEGY—Designing the Data Management Component
Data management approaches

Flat file management

Relational database management

Tables are defined in a database schema

Cut and paste

Select

Project

Join

Normalization

Forms

First normal form

The Attribute value must be atomic

For each Attribute, there is no repetition of values, and no internal data structure

Second normal form

First normal form requirements

Each non-key Attribute describes something identifiable only by the entire key

Third normal form

Second normal form requirements

Each non-key Attribute depends only on the key, and is not just a further description of another non-key Attribute

Fourth normal form

Third normal form requirements

The values of two or more non-key Attributes do not always map to another non-key Attribute

Fifth normal form

Fourth normal form requirements

The values of two or more non-key Attributes do not always map to another non-key Attribute, following a join operation

Price

Increase in the number of tables

Decrease in the match between the tables and problem-domain-based constructs

Performance cost for accessing more tables and for cutting and pasting tables

OO DBMS

Extended relational

Extended OOPL

Assessing data management tools

Designing the Data Management Component

Design the data layout

Flat file

Define first normal form tables

List each Class and its Attributes

Bring that list into first normal form

Define a file for each first normal form table

Measure performance and storage needs

Back off from first normal form to meet performance and storage requirements

If needed, collapse the Attributes for a Gen-Spec Structure into a single file

If needed, combine some Attributes into some sort of encoded value

Flat file, using a tagged specification language

Define a tagged specification language

The language consists of tags, a starting mark, registered items, and an ending mark

Every PDC class gets a "tag name" Attribute and a "how I store myself in the tagged language" Service

Design a parser to reconstitute the tagged language into Objects

Relational

Define third normal form tables

List each Class and its Attributes

Bring that list into third normal form

Define a database table for each third normal form table

Measure and meet performance and storage needs

Object-oriented

Extended relational approach

Extended OOPL approach

There may be no added steps to normalize the Attributes

The database management system itself maps Object values into its storage of those values

Design the corresponding Services

Pattern

Add an Attribute and Service to each Class-&-Object with Objects to be stored

Treat them as an "implicit" Attribute and Service

With this design, an Object will know how to store itself

The "store myself" Attribute and Service form a needed bridge between the PDC and the DMC

With multiple inheritance, such a tag name Attribute and corresponding Service could be defined and then inherited

Flat file

The Object needs to know

Which file(s) to open

How to position the file to the right record

How to retrieve old values (if any)

How to update with new values

Define an ObjectServer Class-&-Object

To tell each Object to save itself

To retrieve stored Objects for use by the other design components

Expect to "batch up" file accessing needs for reasonable performance

Relational

The Object needs to know

Which tables to access

How to access the needed rows

How to retrieve the old values (if any)

How to update with new values

Define an ObjectServer Class-&-Object

To tell each Object to save itself

To retrieve stored Objects for use by the other design components

Object-oriented

Extended relational approach

Extended OOPL approach

No added Services are required

The database management system itself provides the "store yourself" behavior for each Object to be held over time

Save the values of each Object by marking it as needing to be held over time

Bibliography

This bibliography identifies books and articles that have had major impact ("primary bibliography") or some impact ("secondary bibliography") on the development of OOD. An additional section lists helpful reference publications. A final section lists related publications by the authors.

PRIMARY BIBLIOGRAPHY

1. Books

[Apple, 1988] *Human Interface Guidelines: The Apple Desktop Interface.* Addison-Wesley, 1988.

[Cox, 1986] Cox, Brad. *Object-Oriented Programming.* Addison-Wesley, 1986.

[Date, 1986] Date, C. J. *An Introduction to Database Systems*, fourth edition. Addison-Wesley, 1986.

[Digitalk, 1988] *Smalltalk/V Tutorial and Handbook.* Digitalk, Inc., 1988.

[Ellis, 1990] Ellis, Margaret, and Bjarne Stroustrup. *The Annotated C++ Reference Manual.* Addison-Wesley, 1990.

[Ezzell, 1989] Ezzell, Ben. *Object-Oriented Programming in Turbo Pascal 5.5.* Addison-Wesley, 1989.

[Fox, 1990] Fox, Edward A., editor. *Resources in Human-Computer Interaction.* ACM Press, 1990.

[Goldberg, 1989] Goldberg, Adele, and David Robson. *Smalltalk-80: The Language*, Addison-Wesley, 1989.

[Laurel, 1990] Laurel, Brenda, editor. *The Art of Human-Computer Interaction.* Addison-Wesley, 1990.

[Kernighan, 1976] Kernighan, Brian, and Dennis Ritchie. *The C Programming Language*, second edition. Addison-Wesley, 1976.

[Meyer, 1988] Meyer, Bertrand. *Object-Oriented Software Construction.* Prentice Hall, 1988.

[Norman, 1988] Norman, Don. *The Design of Everyday Things.* Doubleday, 1988.

[Parsaye, Chignell, Khoshafian, Wong, 1989] Parsaye, Kamran, Mark Chignell, Setrag Khoshafian, and Harry Wong. *Intelligent Databases*. Wiley, 1989.

[Rubin, 1988] Rubin, Tony. *User Interface Design for Computer Systems*. John Wiley & Sons, 1988.

[Shneiderman, 1987] Shneiderman, Ben. *Designing the User Interface*. Addison-Wesley, 1987.

[Tracz, 1988a] Tracz, Will. *Tutorial: Software Reuse: Emerging Technology*. IEEE, 1988.

[US, 1983] ANSI/MIL-STD-1815A, *Reference Manual for the Ada Programming Language*. Ada Joint Program Office, U.S. Department of Defense, 1983.

2. Articles

[Auer, 1989] Auer, Ken. "Which Object-Oriented Language Should We Choose?" *Hotline on Object-Oriented Technology*. SIGS Publications, November 1989.

[Gomaa, 1989] Gomaa, Hassan. "Structuring Criteria for Real-Time System Design," *ICSE '89 Proceedings*. IEEE/ACM, 1989.

[Nicholson, 1991] Nicholson, Robert T. "Designing a Portable GUI Toolkit," *Dr. Dobbs' Journal*, January 1991.

[Norman, 1990] Norman, Don. "Why Interfaces Don't Work," *The Art of Human-Computer Interaction*, edited by Brenda Laurel. Addison-Wesley, 1990.

[Rheingold, 1990] Rheingold, Howard. "An Interview with Don Norman," *The Art of Human-Computer Interaction*, edited by Brenda Laurel. Addison-Wesley, 1990.

SECONDARY BIBLIOGRAPHY

1. Books

[Boehm, 1981] Boehm, Barry. *Software Engineering Economics*. Prentice Hall, 1981.

[Bouldin, 1989] Bouldin, Barbara. *Agents of Change*. Prentice Hall, 1989.

[Cherry, 1990] Cherry, George. *Software Construction by Object-Oriented Pictures*. Dorset House, 1990.

[DeMarco, 1978] DeMarco, Tom. *Structured Analysis and System Specification.* Prentice Hall, 1978.

[Fisher, 1989] Fisher, Alan S. *CASE: Using Software Development Tools.* John Wiley & Sons, 1988.

[Gardarin, Georges, and Valduriez, 1989] Gardarin, Georges, and Patrick Valduriez. *Relational Databases and Knowledge Bases,* Addison-Wesley, 1989.

[Gilb, 1988] Gilb, Tom. *Principals of Software Engineering Management.* Addison-Wesley, 1988.

[Humphrey, 1989] Humphrey, Watts. *Managing the Software Process.* Addison-Wesley, 1989.

[McClure, 1989] McClure, Carma. *CASE Is Software Automation.* Prentice Hall, 1989.

[Connell and Shafer, 1989] Connell, John L., and Linda Shafer. *Structured Rapid Prototyping.* Prentice Hall, 1989.

2. Articles

[Apple, 1989a] "The Future Belongs to OOP," *Apple Viewpoints,* December 19, 1988.

[Apple, 1989b] "The Power of Object-Oriented Programming," *Apple Direct,* February 1989.

[Banerjee, Chou, Garza, Kim, Woelk, Ballou, 1987] Banerjee, Jay, Hong-Tai Chou, Jorge Garza, Won Kim, Darrell Woelk, and Ballou Nat. "Data Model Issues for Object-Oriented Applications," *ACM Transactions on Office Information Systems,* January 1987.

[Blaha, Premerlani, and Rumbaugh, 1988] Blaha, Michael, William Premerlani, and James Rumbaugh. "Relational Database Design Using an Object-Oriented Methodology," *Communications of the ACM,* April 1988.

[Bloom and Zdonik, 1989] Bloom, Tony, and Stanley Zdonik. "Issues in the Design of Object-Oriented Database Programming Languages," *ACM OOPSLA 87 Proceedings,* October 1987.

[Boehm, 1988] Boehm, Barry. "A Spiral Model of Software Development and Enhancement," *IEEE Computer,* May 1988.

[Boehm, 1988] Boehm, Barry. "Understanding and Controlling Software Costs," *IEEE Transactions on Software Engineering,* October 1988.

[Booch, 1986] Booch, Grady. "Object-Oriented Development," *IEEE Transactions on Software Engineering*, February 1986.

[Brooks, 1988] Brooks, Fred. "No Silver Bullet," *IEEE Software*, April 1988.

[Bruce, 1988] Bruce, Thomas. "CASE Brought Down to Earth," *Database & Programming Design*, October 1988.

[Business Week, 1990] "A New Era for Auto Quality," *Business Week*, October 22, 1990.

[Cattell and Rogers, 1986] Cattell, R., and T. Rogers. "Combining Object-Oriented and Relational Models of Data," *IEEE International Workshop on Object-Oriented Database Systems Proceedings*, 1986.

[Danforth, 1988] Danforth, Scott, and Chris Tomlinson. "Type Theories and Object-Oriented Programming," *ACM Computing Surveys*, March 1988.

[Embley and Woodfield, 1987] Embley, David, and Scott Woodfield. "A Knowledge Structure for Reusing Abstract Data Types," *Proceedings of the Ninth International Conference on Software Engineering*. IEEE, 1987. Also in Tracz [1988a].

[Fischer, 1989] Fischer, Gerhard "Human-Computer Interaction in Software: Lessons Learned, Challenges Ahead," *IEEE Software*, January 1989.

[Hull and King, 1987] Hull, Richard, and Roger King. "Semantic Database Modeling: Survey, Applications, and Research Issues," *ACM Computing Surveys*, September 1987.

[Ingalls, 1981] Ingalls, David. "Design Principles Behind Smalltalk," *Byte*, August 1981.

[Jacobsen, 1987] Jacobsen, Ivar. "Object-Oriented Development in an Industrial Environment," *ACM OOPSLA '87 Proceedings*, October 1987.

[Jalote, 1989] Jalote, Pankaj. "Functional Refinement and Nested Objects for Object-Oriented Design," *IEEE Transactions on Software Engineering*, March 1989.

[Kang, 1987] Kang, Kyo. "Reuse-Based Development Methodology," *Proceedings from the Workshop on Software Reusability and Maintainability*. National Institute of Software Quality and Productivity, 1987. Also in Tracz [1988a].

[Kim, Ballou, Chou, Garza, and Woelk, 1988] Kim, Ballou, Chou, Garza, Woelk. "Integrating an Object-Oriented Programming System with a Database System," *ACM OOPSLA '88 Proceedings*, October 1988.

[Ladden, 1989] Ladden, Richard. "A Survey of Issues to Be Considered in the Development of an Object-Oriented Development Methodology for Ada," *Ada Letters*, March/April 1989.

[Lee, Rissman, D'Ippolito, Plinta, and Scoy, 1988] Lee, Rissman, D'Ippolito, Plinta, Scoy. "An OOD Paradigm for Flight Simulators," *CMU-SEI Technical Report*, second edition, September 1988.

[Loomis, Shaw, and Rumbaugh, 1987] Loomis, M., A. Shah, and J. Rumbaugh. "An Object Modeling Technique for Conceptual Design," *European Conference on OOP*, June 1987.

[Lubars, 1987] Lubars, Mitchell. "Wide-Spectrum Support for Software Reusability," *Proceedings from the Workshop on Software Reusability and Maintainability*. National Institute of Software Quality and Productivity, 1987. Also in Tracz [1988a].

[Lubars, 1988] Lubars, Mitchell. "Code Reusability in the Large versus Code Reusability in the Small," *Tutorial: Software Reuse: Emerging Technology*. IEEE, 1988.

[Miller, 1956] Miller, G. A. "The Magical Number Seven, Plus or Minus Two: Some Limits on Our Capacity for Processing Information," *Psychological Review*, March 1963.

[Miller, 1975] Miller, G. A. "The Magical Number Seven after Fifteen Years," *Studies in Long-Term Memory*, edited by A. Kennedy. Wiley, 1975.

[Millikin, 1989] Millikin, Michael. "Object-Orientation: What It Can Do for You," *Computerworld*, March 13, 1989.

[Norman, 1990] Norman, Ron. "Object-Oriented Analysis & Design," presented at the DPMA Information Technology Conference, San Diego, October 1990.

[Parnas, 1972], Parnas, David. "On the Criteria for Decomposing Programs into Modules," *Communications of the ACM*, December 1972.

[Potter and Trueblood, 1988] Potter, William, and Robert Trueblood. "Traditional, Semantic, and Hyper-Semantic Approaches to Data Modeling," *IEEE Computer*, June 1988.

[Ramamoorthy and Sheu, 1988] Ramamoorthy, C. V., and Phillip Sheu, "Object-Oriented Systems," *IEEE Expert*, Fall 1988.

[Rumbaugh, 1987] Rumbaugh, James. "Relations as Semantic Constructs in an Object-Oriented Language," *ACM OOPSLA '87 Proceedings*, October 1987.

[Seidewitz, 1987] Seidewitz, Ed. "Object-Oriented Programming in Smalltalk and Ada," *ACM OOPSLA '87 Proceedings*, October 1987.

[Seidewitz and Stark, 1987] Seidewitz, Ed, and Mike Stark. "Towards a General Object-Oriented Software Development Methodology," *Ada Letters*, vol. 7, no. 4.

[Simos, 1987] Simos, Mark. "The Domain-Oriented Lifecycle: Towards an Extended Process Model for Reusability," *Proceedings from the Workshop on Software Reusability and Maintainability*, National Institute of Software Quality and Productivity, 1987. Also in Tracz [1988a].

[Smith, 1988] Smith, Connie. "Applying Synthesis Principles to Create Responsive Software Systems," *IEEE Transactions on Software Engineering*, October 1988.

[Smith and Zdonik, 1987] Smith, Karen, and Stanley Zdonik. "Intermedia: A Case Study on the Differences between Relational and Object-Oriented Database Systems," *ACM OOPSLA 87 Proceedings*, September 1987.

[Stankovic, 1988] Stankovic, John. "Misconceptions about Real-Time Computing," *IEEE Computer*, October 1988.

[Stroustrop, 1988a] Stroustrup, Bjarne. "A Better C," *Byte*, August 1988.

[Stroustrup, 1988b] Stroustrup, Bjarne. "What Is Object-Oriented Programming?" *IEEE Software*, May 1988.

[Teorey, 1986] Teorey, T., D. Yang, and J. Fry. "A Logical Design Methodology for Relational Databases Using the Extended Entity-Relationship Model," *ACM Computing Surveys*, June 1986.

[Thomas, 1989] Thomas, Dave. "What's an Object?" *Byte*, March 1989.

[Tracz, 1988b] Tracz, Will. "Confessions of a Used Program Salesman," a series of seven articles from various issues of *IEEE Software*, reprinted in *Tutorial: Software Reuse: Emerging Technology*. IEEE, 1988.

[Tracz, 1988c] Tracz, Will. "RMISE Workshop on Software Reuse Meeting Summary," *Tutorial: Software Reuse: Emerging Technology.* IEEE, 1988. Also in Tracz [1988a].

[Tracz, 1988d] Tracz, Will. "Software Reuse: Motivators and Inhibitors," *Proceedings of COMPCON.* IEEE, Spring 1987. Also in Tracz [1988a]. Also in Tracz [1988a].

[Tracz, 1988e] Tracz, Will. "Software Reuse Myths," ACM SIGSOFT Software Engineering Notes, January 1988. Also in Tracz [1988a].

[Unland and Schlageter, 1989] Unland, R., and G. Schlageter. "An Object-Oriented Programming Environment for Advanced Database Applications," *Journal of Object-Oriented Programming,* May/ June 1989.

[Wegner, 1987] Wegner, Peter. "Dimensions of Object-Based Language Design," *ACM OOPSLA '87 Proceedings,* October 1987.

[Zaniolo, Ait-Kaci, Beech, Cammarata, Kerschberg, Maier, 1986] Zaniolo, Carlo, Hassan Ait-Kaci, David Beech, Stephanie Cammarata, Larry Kerschberg, and David Maier, "Object-Oriented Database Systems and Knowledge Systems," *Expert Database Systems,* edited by Larry Kerschberg, 1986.

3. On-Line Forums

BIX: OOD Conference.

CompuServe: Computer Language Forum.

REFERENCE PUBLICATIONS

[Berryman, 1984] Berryman, Gregg. *Notes on Graphic Design and Visual Communication.* William Kaufmann, 1984.

[Britannica, 1986] *Encyclopaedia Britannica.* Articles on "Behaviour, Animal," "Classification Theory," and "Mood." Encyclopaedia Britannica, Inc., 1986.

[IEEE, 1983] *IEEE Standard Glossary of Software Engineering Terminology* (Standard 729). IEEE, 1983.

[Lanham, 1981] Lanham, Richard A. *Revising Business Prose.* Charles Scribner's Sons, 1981.

[McKenzie, 1980] McKenzie, E. C. *14,000 Quips and Quotes for Writers and Speakers,* "Religion." Outlet Book Company, a Random House

Company, New York. The "Religion" section is a great source of "method" one-liners. Just substitute the word *religion* for the word *method*, and chuckle away! (In a similar fashion, it's also a great source for programming-language jokes.)

[Oxford, 1986] *Dictionary of Computing*. Oxford University Press, 1986.

[Rosenau, 1981] Rosenau, Milton. *Successful Project Management*. Wadsworth, 1981.

[Webster's, 1977] *Webster's New Twentieth-Century Dictionary*, Collins World, 1977.

RELATED PUBLICATIONS

1. Books

[Coad, 1990a] Coad, Peter. *Object-Oriented Analysis*. Seminar notes. Object International, 1990.

[Coad, 1990b] Coad, Peter. *Object-Oriented Design*. Seminar notes. Object International, 1990.

[Coad and Yourdon, 1991] Coad, Peter, and Edward Yourdon. *Object-Oriented Analysis*, second edition. Prentice Hall, 1991.

[Yourdon, 1988a] Yourdon, Edward. *Managing the Structured Techniques*, fourth edition. Prentice Hall, 1988.

[Yourdon and Constantine, 1979] Yourdon, Edward, and Larry Constantine. *Structured Design*. Prentice Hall, 1979.

2. Articles

[Coad, 1991b] Coad, Peter. "Analysis and Design Column," Coad's regular column in *Journal of Object-Oriented Programming*. SIGS Publications, 1991.

[Coad, 1989] Coad, Peter. "OOA: Object-Oriented Analysis," *American Programmer*, Summer 1989.

[Coad and Yourdon, 1990] Coad, Peter, and Edward Yourdon, "OOA—Object-Oriented Analysis," *IEEE Tutorial on System and Software Requirements Engineering*, 1990.

[Yourdon, 1988b] Yourdon, Edward. "More on the Future of CASE," *American Programmer*, October 1988.

[Yourdon, 1988c] Yourdon, Edward. "Sayonara, Structured Stuff," *American Programmer*, August 1988.

Index